BE A
BETTER PILOT

BE A BETTER PILOT

Alan Bramson MRAeS

Chairman of the Panel of Examiners
Liveryman of the Guild of Air Pilots and Air Navigators
Illustrations and photographs by the author

Foreword by Edward G. Tripp
Editor, *AOPA Pilot*

Arco Publishing, Inc.
New York

To my father, Jack.

Published 1980 by Arco Publishing Inc,
219 Park Avenue South, New York, N.Y. 10003

© Alan Bramson 1980

First published in the United Kingdom in 1980
by Martin Dunitz Limited

**Library of Congress Cataloging in Publication
Data**
Bramson, Alan Ellesmere.
  Be a better pilot.
  Includes index.
  1. Airplanes – Piloting. I. Title.
TL710.B62   629.132'5243   80-13401
ISBN 0-668-04901-4

Printed in Canada

CONTENTS

FOREWORD

by Edward G. Tripp, Editor, **AOPA Pilot**

Alan Bramson has developed an enthusiastic following for his writing on aviation over many years. He writes regular articles for flying magazines all over the world including *Pilot* in Great Britain, *Canadian Aviation, Aircraft* (Australia), *World Air News* (South Africa), *AOPA Pilot* and *Flying*. He also has several books to his credit including *Flight Briefing for Pilots* which has now been published in six volumes.

His activity as a flight instructor examiner for the past twenty five years, together with his experience of flight testing numerous new aircraft each year have laid the basis of his extensive aviation knowledge. This, combined with his thought, observation and ability to communicate, ensures that anything written by him is of the greatest practical use to all pilots.

Be a Better Pilot is an exhortation, a challenge and an approach to safe flying which is as applicable to ATPs as it is to fledglings. At the same time as he is imparting information and knowledge Alan Bramson is also projecting something more fundamental to all flying activities – attitude. In covering everything from planning to shut down the author demonstrates the universal principles of aviation and the common concerns of pilots everywhere, no matter what type of flying they do.

Best of all, *Be a Better Pilot* is full of uncomplicated thinking and common sense, which is an education for the beginner and a valuable re-conditioning for the experienced.

PREFACE

Man is an animal of contradictions. He can build bridges, great towns or transport systems and can put a fellow creature on the moon, yet ingenious man is also capable of making self-destructive decisions that even the simplest creatures know how to avoid.

What is it about man that can urge him to drive at high speed in fog, to use powerful machines without a suitable safety guard or to continue flying in weather that is beyond both his own capabilities and those of his aircraft? Part of the answer to this complex question is lack of awareness, something civilization has tamed out of the human species. But the less flattering ingredient is clearly stupidity and lack of self-discipline, two characteristics of potential danger in those who fly.

At risk of sounding defeatist I must say that, although the stupid can be educated, in my experience there is very little that can be done about the indisciplined. Nothing will prevent the lunatic fringe from driving at high speed in fog and any reader who, deep down, recognizes himself as such a character is advised to put down this book now. There is little point in reading on for he is hardly likely to accept my advice which would be to give up flying and stick to golf.

To the keen, balanced, and conscientious pilot who recognizes his limitations and wishes to do better for his own safety and enjoyment I hasten to explain that this is not simply a book telling you how to deal with emergencies. Its aim is rather to develop habits and techniques that will prevent the real emergency and all the risks it entails from arising.

I do not claim to have invented the many practices described here. They find their origins in some of the finest flying training establishments, civil and military, where the experience of talented pilots acquired over many years has been distilled into wisdom.

For the past twenty-five years I have tested flying instructors for the issue and renewal of their ratings and during that period I have naturally come face to face with many of the weaknesses and problem areas that can, in time, be guaranteed to cause an accident. Much of this experience is reflected in this book. You could argue that the accident rate in private and general aviation is remarkably good. While this might be true when the statistics are compared with motor cycling, mountaineering and some other activities, most fatal aviation accidents need never have happened had the pilots concerned shown a little more respect for the privileged environment of the air. Not everyone is fortunate enough to fly and certainly I have always regarded it as a privilege that my health, capabilities and time in history have allowed me to take a small part in the wonderful world of aeronautics.

If I were to single out one ingredient above all others that poses a constant danger to so many pilots it is lack of professionalism. There are, of course, those who do not aspire to be professional about anything and indeed I would be the first to leap to the defence of weekend pilots with ambitions that are confined to flying around the local airfield on a fine Sunday morning. There is nothing wrong with that provided those who have confined their proficiency to 'sunny Sundays' do not venture into the totally different world of flying in heavy traffic or under IMC. These conditions demand professionalism, even from the amateurs. It is hard to put across this lesson to those not earning a living as pilots because in so many activities a lack of professionalism does not mean the end of the world. In tennis or golf, for example, the worst that can happen is that you will lose the game. Be unprofessional in aviation and sooner or later you may break your neck and hit the newspaper headlines in the process.

When writing a book of this kind it is convenient to use the words 'he' and 'his'. However there are these days many women pilots and it is not uncommon for them to reach the top echelons of professional and sporting aviation. So to them I say please read 'she' in place of 'he' and 'her' instead of 'his'. This book is of course for women as much as for men.

In the course of writing 'how-to' articles for aviation magazines throughout the world I have met a constant demand for more information of this practical kind. It is this demand that has inspired *Be a better pilot*. If I have been unable to deal with every aspect of good airmanship in this book I can at least hope that the various common sense procedures in the text will encourage the reader to think in such a way that he takes nothing for granted and takes account of what might happen in this imperfect world. He will then be equipped to deal with the unexpected and this is the most crucial skill of all. Because it is the unexpected that produces the kind of situation in which every amateur pilot must fly like a professional.

A. E. B. July 1979

12

1. INTRODUCTION

It is often claimed that there is nothing wrong with aircraft; it is only when you sit a pilot behind the controls that the hardware becomes potentially dangerous. Like all generalizations this one is not entirely true. Not all accidents are the fault of the pilot and many good pilots devote a lifetime to flying as professionals or amateurs without so much as scratching the paint.

At the other end of the scale are the tearaways, the lunatic fringe of aviation who are not fit to be let loose on a bicycle in open country, let alone in an aircraft. 'Who gives these people a pilot's licence?' you may ask, but it is no use pointing the finger at instructors or the licensing authorities. From first-hand experience I can tell you that a pilot under test for a rating may behave in a normal, rational manner, as clearly he is on his best behaviour while in the presence of the instructor. But what some of these worthies get up to when the sobering eye of authority is out of sight is another matter. The obviously unbalanced person is no problem to the examiner – it is written all over the candidate's face and confirmed by the way he reacts under test. Unfortunately the real danger is sometimes not a wild man at all. There may be nothing more seriously wrong with him than a lack of awareness and a touch of laziness, a belief that second best will do. As he has no ambitions to earn a living in aviation he considers that checks and vital actions are for the airline pilot, not him. 'Besides,' he will add, 'it's only a light 'plane and people are flying them every day of the week.' What these people fail to recognize is that you may kill yourself just as easily in a 100hp trainer as you can in a jet fighter.

In many respects we are dealing with a human problem in the case of the irresponsible pilot. In other walks of life his actions may result in nothing more serious than letting someone down, forgetting to buy the fish on the way home from the office or getting wet because a black sky did not encourage him to wear a raincoat. All that may be part of an 'easy come easy go' way of life, something to laugh about later. In the aviation environment such an attitude will sooner or later lead to a 'situation' and when the situation is wrongly handled it can so easily become an accident. For, to quote an old saying, an aircraft is a good servant but a bad master. It will serve you well as long as it is kept under strict control and made to fly according to the rules of aviation. But let it take over, break the rules or ignore the warning signs and the aircraft will bite the hand that should be its master.

Typical attitudes and malpractices that so often contribute to a serious accident are:

a) Failure to plan the flight.

b) 'Pre-flight checks are a drag so let's not bother.'

c) Insufficient knowledge of the aircraft and a refusal to obtain this knowledge on grounds that when you've flown one type you have flown them all.

d) An unshakeable belief held by some people that they are 'ace' pilots when in fact their capabilities are below average or even worse.

e) Get-home-itis.

Any one of these factors can lead to disaster (some of them often have) but they are not problems caused by lack of intelligence on the part of the pilots concerned. On the contrary, pilots who get themselves in at the deep end are often intelligent people. Normally such habits do not result from sub standard training, because by the time a pilot is in a position to fly off somewhere on his own or with friends he must have gained at least a Private Pilot's Licence and that means he has passed the written examination papers and the flying test. No, these problems exist in the men themselves and in some cases nothing anyone can say will prevent men from killing themselves one day. Unfortunately others sometimes suffer as a result.

You think I exaggerate? Well, I have known of a case where a man with a coronary condition who had already suffered several heart attacks managed to obtain a PPL by going to a different doctor and bending the rules. This story could have had an even worse ending. In fact he died at the controls while taxiing out to take-off. Fortunately his schoolboy son, who was in the aircraft with him, switched off the engine before the 'plane took over. This does not stop one wondering what could lead a man who had suffered heart attacks to risk not only his own life but also his son's.

Not so very long ago two men took off in a single-engine light 'plane to fly across the English Channel. Fog was reported over the sea and they were advised to wait. Neither pilot had any instrument flying experience but the aircraft had a flight panel and VHF/VOR and they set off regardless. Half way across the Channel they encountered fog and appeals for radar steers came over the radio. It is often the practice to record radio conversations and on the tape can clearly be heard the urgent voice of the pilot in the right-hand seat saying 'Watch your Sperry, watch your Sperry.' They were never seen again. What encourages a man without instrument flying experience to take off and fly into known fog?

I have sometimes asked myself another question. Had I been there and strongly advised them to wait for the fog to blow away would they have taken any notice of me? Perhaps yes – perhaps no, depending on human factors again. Those who have been warned by others that they are heading for an accident and have behaved in the foolhardy way I have described will probably gain nothing from reading this book. Nothing I can say will stop the inevitable from happening. But those readers with open minds who have knowingly pushed their luck, have thought about it since and who feel a little uncomfortable about one or two of the things I have mentioned will certainly benefit from a course on sound airmanship – an old fashioned term which is, nonetheless more important today than ever it was.

For pilots with limited experience here are the main human factors likely to interfere with the sound judgement essential to good airmanship:

1. Laziness

2. False pride

3. Over-confidence

4. Haste

5. Lack of awareness

6. Carelessness

These factors can be related to the items listed on page 14. 'Failure to plan the flight' usually stems from the mistaken belief that everything will be alright – the weather is OK at the moment, there are instruments and radio in the aircraft (although maybe the pilot does not know how to use them properly) and if the weather does get rough you can always turn back (although too often pride says 'press on').

Pre-flight checks will be dealt with in the next chapter but at this stage it is sufficient to say that the seeds of an accident are almost invariably sown on the ground, often as a result of neglecting this particular aspect of airmanship.

The great majority of motorists have little knowledge of how their car actually works. There was a time when the private pilot prided himself that what was good enough for the car driver rated zero in aviation. Not for him the can't-tell-a-kingpin-from-a-conrod approach; he had a good working knowledge of both engine and airframe. Of course many aspects of flying have over the years become increasingly complex but regrettably not all pilots have felt moved to face the challenge. Consequently you can meet pilots of light aircraft, even complex twins, who know disturbingly little about the hardware, its safety features, limitations and basic servicing requirements. Sometimes this ignorance occurs because the pilot concerned is beaten before he starts. 'I am no good at technical things' he will tell you. So instead of trying to understand what are, in the main, straight-forward features of the aircraft, he learns the information parrot fashion, never really understands it and therefore forgets it after passing the examinations for his licence or rating.

There is, of course, no law against ignorance (except ignorance of the law itself). But in flying ignorance paves the way to disaster. You may lead a charmed life flying a simple 'plane without knowing how this or that should be operated. But the mistaken belief that 'if you've flown one type of aircraft, you have flown them all' will almost certainly lead to trouble when you aspire to faster, more complex types. I have met pilots who were not sure how to select 'crossfeed' in the event of engine failure, who thought the vacuum pump drain was for running off the engine oil, and who lost the use of their airspeed indicator in icing conditions because they did not know how to operate the pitot heater. Misuse of the carburettor heat control would likewise fill a book. Aircraft are not all the same. Some are more different than others and a calculated aversion to all things technical, however simple, can only lead to trouble.

The 'ace' complex is an interesting one. In real life few airplane drivers are aces yet one only has to put up a few tents at the local airfield, hang out the odd flag, then invite in the public and almost overnight many normally quite retiring flying men fancy themselves as demonstration pilots. Air display flying is not for everyone, even experienced pilots. It is a special art in its own right. You may be a proficient aerobatic pilot at 4000ft but come the day when without practice you elect to do a show on the deck and there will certainly be surprises in abundance. For example, in place of that nice, clearly defined horizon as you roll off the top of a loop will be trees, roof tops and perhaps lines of washing in people's back gardens. A slow roll at even 1000ft is quite a leisurely affair and who cares if you lose several hundred feet while inverted. Try the same manoeuvre low down; the ground rushes by and a height loss followed by a sudden full stop in the inverted position, while guaranteed to be the highlight of the show, will earn you no more than a headline in the local paper.

The case of the Vintage Fly Past during the annual Biggin Hill Air Display near London illustrates the risks of poor pilot technique. I remember speaking to the owner of an immaculate Gipsy Moth, built in

1928 and gleaming like a new pin. He confided that the previous day while watching the other aircraft in the fly past and trying to hold position his attention had wandered and he almost stalled in front of the crowd. I warned him that the presence of spectators and a public address system did not mean he was an experienced demonstration pilot and that he should fly his Moth at a safe airspeed. On the next fly past he spun in over the trees, destroying the priceless Gipsy Moth, although fortunately with little damage to himself. It could have been a lot worse but that man almost had to kill himself to discover he was no 'ace'. Display flying is a very special skill. It has to be learned, practised and developed like any other.

A more common manifestation of the 'ace' complex is an all too common disregard for the weather which takes the form of 'get-home-itis'. When it comes to fooling around in bad weather, man is in a class of his own. Most creatures have a built-in warning system which tells them when to take cover. Mankind, or a section of it, is sometimes too stupid to come in out of the rain. Let me quote some examples.

The pilot of a light aircraft took off from an airfield near London, leaving behind a vague message to the effect that he would be back before dark. With him was his young son. There was no Avgas at the destination, which turned out to be a disused airfield, so he obtained cans of motor fuel from a nearby garage and topped up his tanks. By now his plans were behind schedule and it was obvious he could not get himself back to London before dark. Furthermore a telephone call to the nearest met. office revealed strong risk of snow showers and moderate icing. The light 'plane had no pitot heat, no instrument lighting and only a simple VHF transceiver yet he elected to attempt the journey home. On the way he ran into snow, lost visual contact with the ground and called up for help. Later they found the wreckage of his aircraft floating in the Bristol Channel.

A famous personality with something of a reputation for getting there, come hail, rain, fog or snow, took off in his light twin to fly home. Many of the airfields in his part of the world were reporting visibilities of 200m, that for his destination being even less. Not far away an airport with full ILS/Radar facilities was reporting 1000m but the pilot elected to carry on and land at base where his car was parked. The home airfield had no approach aids, not even VDF, and the one short runway was surrounded by power lines, trees, built-up areas and the like. As he approached the runway threshold he flew into higher ground killing himself and the five passengers.

These are just two examples of situations where the desire to get home so clouded judgement that, in the first case, an aircraft without lighting or ice protection was flown in freezing conditions at night, and in the second, the pilot was experienced, but chose to land at a small airfield when the visibility was no more than a quarter of that laid down for a much more experienced airline crew flying the best equipment available into a modern international airport offering all the aids in the book.

'Get-home-itis' is a very dangerous frame of mind. It must be resisted at all costs. Your car may be waiting for you at the home airfield but a diversion to safe landing conditions will save your life for the cost of a taxi ride and perhaps a late arrival at that dinner party.

After reading this chapter the reader may feel that he should never have taken up flying, that the risks are too high and that it is a thoroughly dangerous activity. Not a bit of it. In fact flying is basically a safe occupation provided one remembers that it will not suffer fools. Obey the rules and you will live to be an old pilot with a fund of happy memories to look back upon. Break the rules and you are a candidate for a different pair of wings – the type that is usually issued with a harp.

As I said earlier in this book, the know-it-all pilot is in most cases beyond help. So is the lunatic fringe. But to the great mass of average pilots who genuinely want to improve their skills there are all manner of techniques and practices that can give flying a new dimension, radically enhance safety and turn even a PPL holder into a professional. Some of these practices are small things, others demand tuition and practice, but in total they represent the cheapest and most effective insurance available.

2. PREPARATION BEFORE FLIGHT

Most people going on holiday take the trouble to pack their bits and pieces some hours before departure. The more practical even give thought to what might go wrong – airsickness on the trip, an upset stomach caused by strange food in a foreign country or red, white and blue lumps from insect bites – and so they may include travel sickness pills, antihistamine cream and the like. All this is a sensible way of preparing for the abnormal.

The worst that can happen to those holidaymakers who do not make intelligent preparations for their vacation is they may be sick on the flight there and back, an upset stomach could make them the fastest runner in the hotel and bites from some strange, multi-engined insect may raise multi-coloured lumps. In contrast, when a pilot shows aversion to planning or preparation the risks he runs are many and, in some cases, dramatic. The engine may stop at a particularly embarrassing moment; he might run out of fuel in the middle of nowhere; or an enforced change of plan due to adverse weather could get him lost, because the one and only map carried in the aircraft covers a big area to the left of track, but not that to the right where the sky is brighter.

Preparation before a holiday (or any other event) is certainly prudent and sensible. Preparation before flight is absolutely vital. It falls under two headings: 1. Flight planning and 2. Pre-flight inspection of the aircraft.

Planning the flight

Weather checks

There was a time when stall/spin incidents used to be top of the fatal accident lists in most countries, but in more recent years this dubious distinction has gone to Weather Induced Accidents (to use the official terminology). The subject of weather appreciation and dealing with IMC will be dealt with in Chapter 7 but at this stage I am assuming that the pilot has a healthy respect for the weather and recognizes his own limitations as well as those of his aircraft.

Imagine you and your friends are of a mind to fly from the local airfield to Funfield, a trip likely to last about two hours, and taking you over varying terrain. A telephone call from home to the local met. man is the first step because what he has to say will enable you to decide if you should indeed visit the airfield or if it would be more sensible to forget aviation that day. You want to know a lot more than what they are reporting locally. Weather information essential to a safe flight is:

1. Actual weather at point of departure and, if you intend to return later that day, forecast weather for the period. It might be CAVOK when you leave but the birds could be walking when you try to return.

2. Route forecast for the period. If you are a strictly VMC pilot, cloud ceilings are important because if, for example, there is a 3000ft mountain en route that rises into a cloud base hovering at 2500ft you will have to plan your flight very intelligently.

3. Actual reports or forecasts for the destination.

4. Actual reports or forecasts for the alternates in case the intended destination closes in.

5. Freezing levels and icing index. Even instrument rated pilots must give serious regard to these because the best pilot in the world will

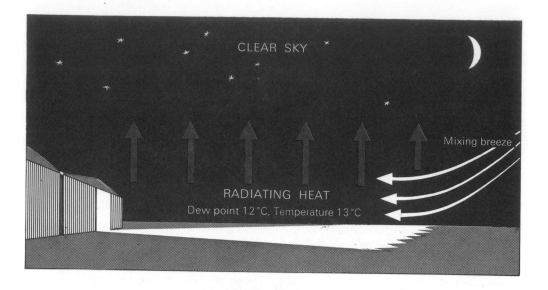

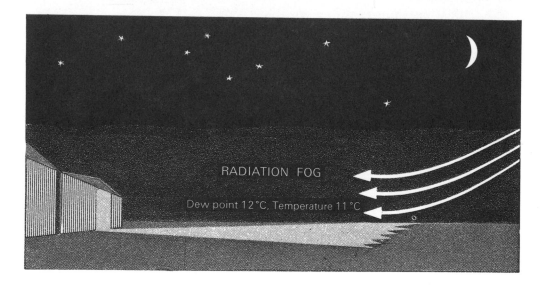

Fig.1: Formation of radiation fog. Upper drawing shows heat radiating into space and mixing breeze. Lower picture illustrates early stages of fog which will mix and thicken with time.

find himself in serious trouble if his aircraft is without ice protection, and he is unable either to descend out of the freezing level because of high terrain or to climb above it for lack of power.

6. Temperature and dew point. This is particularly important at the destination, because a dew point of, say, $+12°C$ and a temperature of $+13°C$ means it has only to get a little colder and there will probably be fog. Fig. 1 shows that, in the presence of a gentle breeze, a clear sky at sundown will allow heat to radiate into space and the resultant drop in temperature will cause the air to become saturated, producing radiation fog.

Planning the route

The shortest distance between two points may be a straight line but that does not automatically mean this is the best route to take. Weather considerations apart, it is common prudence to avoid overflying mountainous areas which are high enough to reduce safe terrain clearance. This is particularly important when there are strong winds because there is the very real danger of encountering severe downdraughts, some of sufficient intensity to cause serious loss of height to a low powered light 'plane. Then again in the right wind and moisture conditions mountains are great producers of cloud and, on cold days, ice. So, unless you are flying a pressurized aircraft or prepared to wear oxygen in a turbocharged non-pressurized 'plane, go round the mountains when the weather is other than ideal. Another fifteen minutes added to the journey time is better than the risks of coming down in the mountains. Even if you survive a forced landing in hostile surroundings the odds are they may never find you. The route should therefore be chosen with regard to:

1. Terrain to be crossed in relation to the capabilities of the aircraft.

2. Areas of controlled airspace to be avoided or, in the case of suitably rated pilots, to be made use of.

3. Availability of suitable radio aids.

4. Weather.

Crossing the sea

A word about flights over water in single-engine aircraft. Without doubt modern piston-engines, particularly those of modest power and simple design, are very reliable. However, it is a fact of aviation life that occasionally an engine does stop. Causes range from simple fuel starvation to more dramatic problems, such as connecting rod failure or bearing trouble (fire is fortunately very rare). What happens when the one and only donkey quits over water depends on many things – wind direction and strength, state of the sea, relationship of swell and wind and, most important, type of aircraft. The trouble with ditching is that it is not an exercise one can practise in realistic terms as one can engine failure after take-off or stalling. Most of our knowledge in the General Aviation field must therefore come from people who have had the experience and lived to tell the tale. In general it would appear that mid-wing aircraft with retractable landing gear (e.g. Piper Aerostar) enter the water best, while the much more popular, fixed nosewheel types with high wings do worst. This book is not a manual of emergency procedures so I shall not explain ditching other than to make these comments on over-water flying in single-engine aircraft:

1. Plan the trip so that water crossings are reduced to the minimum distance practicable.

2. If the journey is away from shipping lanes or small boat traffic carry an inflatable dinghy and
    a) be sure it is in good condition;
    b) be sure you know how to use it;
    c) stow the dinghy where it can be reached in a ditching emergency.
   The carrying of a dinghy large enough for all occupants of the aircraft is particularly important when the water is known to be cold. More people die in the water through hypothermia than as a result of drowning.

3. For all water crossings wear lifejackets and
    a) be sure they are servicable;

  b) be sure you and your passengers know how to use them in an
     emergency.
There is no point in throwing the rolled up lifejackets into the
baggage compartment and then covering them with luggage. In a
ditching there will be no time to sort things out.

4. Even when there is no legal obligation to file a flight plan, always
    do so when you are planning a water crossing, or at least book out
    at the airfield and let your intentions be known. You could be glad
    to know they are looking for you as you bob up and down in the sea
    while the tail of your wonderplane sinks beneath the waves. Not
    many modern aircraft, even light twins, float for more than a few
    minutes. So, even if a ditching following engine failure may be very
    unlikely, it is good airmanship to be prepared.

Selecting the radio facilities

In some parts of the world navaids are few and unreliable. Europe and
North America, however, abound in conveniently placed radio facilities
and, provided the aircraft is equipped to take advantage of VOR, DME
and ADF the task of navigating has never been easier. The problem is that
navigation, for all the obstacles that have mushroomed throughout the
airspace such as airways, prohibited areas, control zones etc., is now so easy
that some pilots have become complacent. They jump in, start up and
blast off without any of the pre-flight preparation I have been advocating
in this chapter. One of the most common malpractices among pilots is to
use outdated charts. These often show the wrong radio frequences and it is
part of Murphy's Law that the very VOR/DME (VORTAC in the USA)
you want to use is sure to be the one they have changed. So in planning the
flight:

1. Make sure the charts are current.

2. List all the frequencies and their identification letters.

3. Be prepared to use another radio facility in case the ideal one is out
    of service.

Selecting the alternates

In an ideal world we would leave base and fly to the destination every time. But life is not like that and, on occasions, there is need for a change in plan. After take-off the place where you had intended to land may close in, a revolution could start there (not unlikely in some parts of the world) or a minor engine or airplane malfunction might necessitate an unscheduled landing. Weather considerations are the most common cause of a diversion, sometimes forcing you to alter heading to an airfield better equipped for instrument approaches, so it is vital to select alternates when planning the flight. Obviously these should be within the range of the aircraft, and when a front is expected to move through, bringing with it weather that is below your limits or those of the aircraft, you must take this weather movement into account in making your selection. Frequencies relating to the alternates should be listed on the flight plan.

Fuel calculations

For peace of mind there is nothing like starting the flight with full tanks. However, it is not always possible to take on maximum fuel because most modern touring singles, and probably all of the twins, can be either full tanks or full cabin aircraft, but not both at the same time.

Some overloaded singles fly quite well, apparently suffering no more than a modest decrease in cruising speed and a reduced rate of climb. However, an overloaded aircraft will be flying with reduced structural safety factors and the practice of ignoring the maximum take-off weight is a dangerous one, particularly in the case of multi-engined types. Most light twins have only marginal engine-out climbing performance and this is rapidly eroded when the aircraft is overweight.

In calculating fuel requirement estimate the flight time, allowing for diversions and a forty-five minute hold, convert this into gallons burned (i.e. time of flight × gallons per hour for the cruise setting to be used) and write the figure down. Next calculate the fuel required with a computer, allowing for engine start, taxiing, take-off and climb. Then compare the result with your estimate. In this way you will recognize at once if you have been accidentally working in the wrong units or using the distance in nautical miles as the groundspeed for the trip.

A typical method of computing fuel requirement involves using the consumption figures provided in the aircraft manual for each phase of flight and listing them as follows:

Engine start, taxi and take-off	1.50
Climb to cruising level	2.00
Diversion: 0.33 hours at 8.5gph.	2.80
Cruise: 4.9 hours at 8.5gph.	41.65
45 minutes hold at 7gph.	5.25
Descent, approach and landing, etc.	1.50
Total fuel	54.70 gallons

A 10 per cent allowance for unexpected headwinds would bring that up to 60 gallons and at the same time provide the pilot with a little peace of mind.

Weight and balance

The smaller and simpler light aircraft are almost impossible to load in an out-of-balance condition. But as one moves on to larger designs (six seats and more) so the opportunities for flying outside the permitted centre of gravity range present themselves. The consequences of overloading have already been mentioned on the previous page but the effects of flying out of balance are rather more subtle.

In simple terms, stability in pitch increases as the centre of gravity is moved forward. You do not get anything for nothing in aeronautics and, as stability in pitch improves, so the degree of pitch control tends to decline. When the centre of gravity is allowed to move aft the reverse occurs; there is an increase in controlability but a marked decline in stability. Furthermore if the centre of gravity is moved back (by incorrect loading of passengers or freight etc.) the moment arm through which both elevators and rudder exert their influence is shortened (Fig. 2) and we now have the worst of two worlds. Because of the aft centre of gravity and its effect on stability the aircraft will more readily go into a spin if mishandled; and, in addition, the shortened moment arm illustrated in Fig. 2 will reduce the effectiveness of the tail surfaces (particularly the rudder) which must first curtail the yaw if there is to be a proper spin recovery.

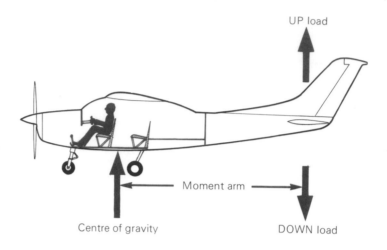

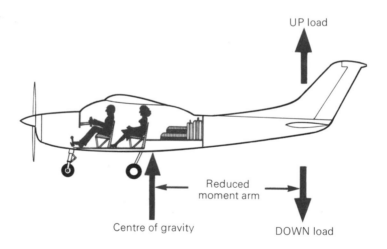

Fig. 2: The effect of centre of gravity on the tail surface moment arm.
     Top aircraft: Forward C of G
     Lower aircraft: Aft C of G

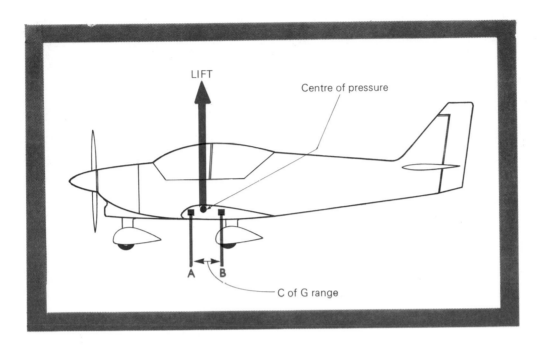

Fig. 3: Centre of gravity range.

For an aircraft to fly properly its total lift (acting through the centre of pressure) must oppose the centre of gravity, the ideal relationship being lift slightly behind weight as shown in Fig. 3. Obviously it is impossible to fix the centre of gravity in one position because fuel is burned off in flight and passenger, freight and baggage loads vary from day to day. Also the centre of pressure moves with changes in angle of attack. Consequently the manufacturers designate a centre of gravity range or, as it is often known, Centre of Gravity Envelope, for safe flight.

Unfortunately there is no uniform system of computing balance but a popular method entails referring to graphs and diagrams provided in the aircraft manual, setting down the figures obtained on a Weight and Balance Form (sometimes called a Load Sheet) and adding up the total weight to see that it does not exceed the maximum authorized for take-off. The moments (i.e. weight in each station or position within the aircraft × its distance from the datum which is defined by the manufacturers) are

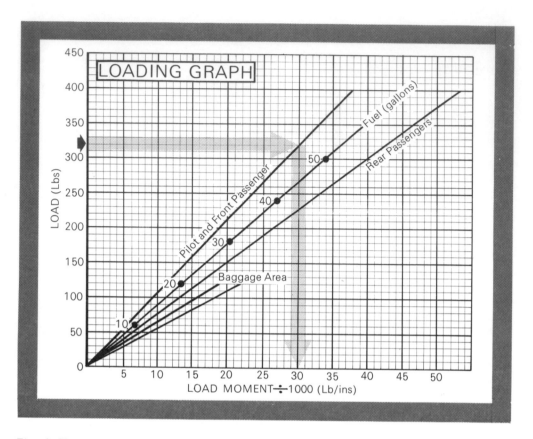

Fig. 4: Typical Loading Graph. The example shows a load moment of 300,000lb/in when the pilot and the front passenger weigh a total of 320lb.

referred to a Centre of Gravity Moment Envelope provided in the manual.

Methods of showing the distance between datum and the various stations range from tiny drawings with figures too small to read with the naked eye (this one is used by manufacturers of larger aircraft that offer more opportunities for misloading than little ones!) to clear simple Loading Graphs of the type illustrated in Fig. 4. Such an arrangement is ideal for relatively small aircraft with up to three rows of seats. It will be seen that one line is devoted to each station and it is a simple matter to trace the weight horizontally to the relevant station diagonal and then drop down to the 'load moment' figure at the bottom of the graph. Once found, the various moments are written on to a Load Sheet and added up. The total moments may then be related to the Centre of Gravity Moment Envelope printed in the manual.

Much of the foregoing should have been learned at the flying schools but sometimes it is left to the student pilot to find out for himself. I often meet pilots who are not entirely sure about how to check weight and balance and consequently brief notes have been included in this chapter, but the basic message is, that you should know your aircraft manual and learn how *not* to load the hardware as well as how it should be done, so that you can take off without fear of entering an almost immediate loop – yes, it has happened.

Filing flight plans

Many years ago it was decided by far-thinking minds that aviation was bigger than nations, and that therefore a central organization should open shop where the aviating states could foregather to agree on standard terminology and procedures. It was a great idea except that members of the International Civil Aviation Organization (ICAO) were free to disregard the majority decision and go their own way. So, nations being what they are, we are left with a degree of uniformity and a number of sometimes quite irrational exceptions. Consequently it is impossible to generalize about legal obligations on filing flight plans because the details differ from country to country. One can, however, say that there is never anything to stop a pilot filing a flight plan for any VFR flight, and if your trip entails flying over sparsely populated areas, water, forest or mountains, it is the height of folly not at least to make your intentions known before departure. In the USA a VFR flight plan is transmitted to the destination and if the aircraft does not arrive (or let its position be known) within thirty minutes of ETA search and rescue operations are started. But if no-one is aware that you may be sitting in the dinghy beating off the fish who is to know where to look for you. The pilot who regards the need to file a flight plan (or at least to book out at the point of departure) as an invasion of his privacy should take himself on one side and ask how he can be helped in an emergency if he deliberately makes the task impossible.

Pre-flight checks

In essence the pre-flight checks can be divided into three parts:

1. The walk-around when the airplane is inspected for obvious damage, followed by an internal check of the flight deck.

2. The instrument, brake and ground manoeuvering checks while taxiing to the holding point.

3. The power checks to ensure proper function of the engine(s), propeller(s) and related instruments.

In my experience power checks are usually done in a haphazard way, instrument checks are often forgotten while taxiing out, and the walk-around, if it is done at all, represents something like a dash to catch the morning train.

Checklists or mnemonics?

Much controversy exists about checklists. Some people are of the opinion that they are an altogether admirable invention while others are only prepared to use them on occasions.

In complex aircraft checklists are a must, but a word of warning here. For some years now it has been the fashion to copy the airline pilots even when flying a 100hp two-seat trainer. There are dangers to this. It should be remembered that most flights by bigger aircraft are two-crew (or more) operations where one pilot or the flight engineer reads out the item and another does the check. It is fine for a single-handed pilot to use a checklist, provided he follows it with discipline. He must avoid at all costs doing some of the checks from memory using mnemonics while using the checklist in a half-hearted manner. That way important items are missed.

The modern pilot has been brought up on checklists but, properly used, there are certain advantages in mnemonics for single-crew operation. These too must be applied correctly. (A number of examples are shown later in the text.)

The walk-around

Items to be checked are listed in the flight manual so the following text is only concerned with general principles.

The purpose of the walk-around is to check for the obvious. You are not carrying out an engineer's inspection. The process starts as you approach the aircraft, since it is easiest to see if the aircraft looks normal from afar. If one wing is down there could be a flat tyre, a damaged or below-pressure strut or something more serious such as structural distortion. Check the positioning of the aircraft and, if it is likely to blow debris into someone's office or at another 'plane, move it by hand.

Far and away the most common fault during the walk-around is failure to check the magneto switches. This is the first thing to do because, until all the switches are off and the mixture is in the ICO (idle cut-off) position, that aircraft is lethal to anyone standing near the propeller(s).

While you are at the cabin door checking the switches turn on the anti-collision beacon or strobe lights. See if they are working. Also switch on the pitot heat, leave it a few seconds, then feel that the pressure tube is getting warm. And while the master switch is on, try the stall warning vane. If you do not check these things now they are certain to be neglected after you have tied yourself into the seat. When flying at night the navigation lights (known as position lights in the USA) should also be checked.

Before turning off the master switch take a look at the fuel gauges so that you can compare their readings with what you see in the tanks during the walk-around.

Most flight manuals include a walk-around diagram such as that illustrated in Fig. 5 and it is only included here because some pilots are not entirely clear about the order of inspection. The idea is to start at the point of entry and walk right round (usually in a clockwise direction) checking flaps, ailerons, wing tips, lights, landing gear, wheels, fuel contents, propeller state, oil level, tail surfaces, static vents/pressure tubes and general airplane condition. A wrinkled fuselage skin above the wing could mean that someone has dropped the bird from a great height during landing.

The best way to avoid forgetting something is to become a creature of habit. While most manuals show a clockwise walk-around, others, for reasons best known to themselves, go for an anti-clockwise circuit of the

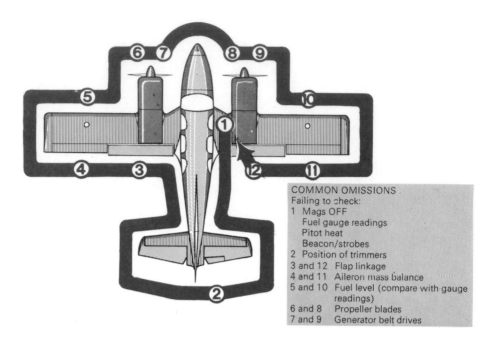

COMMON OMISSIONS
Failing to check:
1 Mags OFF
    Fuel gauge readings
    Pitot heat
    Beacon/strobes
2 Position of trimmers
3 and 12 Flap linkage
4 and 11 Aileron mass balance
5 and 10 Fuel level (compare with gauge
                    readings)
6 and 8 Propeller blades
7 and 9 Generator belt drives

Fig. 5: Typical pre-flight walk-around.

machinery (the excuse that the door is on the other side is, frankly, rubbish). In such cases, beware – habit is broken and you must stick carefully to the checklist even if you are used to walk-arounds.

Although few manuals mention it on most aircraft one can see a lot more of the linkage and hinge mechanism when the flaps are partly lowered. This also demonstrates that they both come down together and are unlikely to provoke an involuntary slow roll on the approach.

A common habit among some pilots is to grab the first aileron encountered on the walk-around and wag it vigorously up and down in an attempt to prove that nothing is going to drop off. There is nothing wrong in *gently* moving the ailerons but no attempt should be made to do this until you reach the other side of the aircraft. By then you will be certain that when you move one aileron the other is not being battered against a step ladder (no doubt left there for the purpose) or part of another aircraft which has been badly parked.

Ice

An aircraft parked overnight at certain times of the year can collect hoar frost on the wings and tail surfaces. It is not generally realized that this, even though it is often quite a thin film, can so disturb the boundary layer that a take-off is impossible. It is an essential part of the walk-around to clear all parts of the flying surfaces (windscreen, static vents etc.) of ice.

Fuel contamination

To remove condensed water, which forms in partly filled fuel tanks and then sinks to the bottom, the 'plane is provided with one or more drain valves, depending on its design. It is a common practice to open the drainer (sometimes known as a strainer) and let the fuel pour on to the ground. The small lake that forms is then touched with the finger which in turn is passed to the nose. At that stage the fuel expert pronounces 'it's petrol' as if he might have expected it to be gin or scotch. This procedure proves nothing. Only by using a clear plastic sampler, which should be kept in the aircraft, is it possible to see:

   a) if sediment or other foreign matter is present;

   b) if all water has been drained. (Water, being heavier than fuel, will sink to the bottom while the coloured Avgas floats to the top.)

Warning: If the vents on the fuel tanks get blocked it is possible, with the fuel selector in the OFF position, to cause back pressure in the tank and fuel lines. Flow from a partly closed drain valve could then cease, and a pilot, believing that he had closed the valve properly would lose a good deal of fuel through the part-opened drain. It is therefore essential to check that fuel drainers close properly after use and, to avoid risk of back pressure, it is good practice to select fuel ON ALL TANKS (if possible) before the walk-around.

Taxi checks

When the nosewheel is directly linked to the pilot's pedals your first opportunity to check that full rudder movement is available will come while taxiing out to the holding point. Before making turns on the ground be sure it is clear to do so. Instrument checks are as follows:

Turning left
Compass and DI (DG in the USA) decreasing
Turn needle to the LEFT
Ball to the RIGHT

Turning right
Compass and DI increasing
Turn needle to the RIGHT
Ball to the LEFT

Other flight instruments
Artificial Horizon (altitude director) erect
VSI zero
Altimeter steady on correct reading

Power checks

Pilots of turboprop or jet aircraft have little to do by way of engine checks other than to monitor the temperatures and pressures during light-up and, in some turboprops, release the fine pitch locks. Piston-engines are a different matter and it is generally accepted that they are less reliable than turbines. Since impending trouble can sometimes be detected before take-off the run-up has, over many years past, become an essential ritual.

Before moving off for the holding point all magneto switches should be switched OFF then ON for the purpose of confirming that the magnetos are working. You are not looking for an RPM drop at this stage (although many pilots mistakenly do) but if a magneto is not working there is little point in taxiing out.

Warm-up time for the engines will depend on the outside temperature but the manual will give guidance here. The aircraft should be headed into wind with the nosewheel straight and for the run-up an area should be chosen that is free of loose stones. Propeller blade damage can be expensive.

By this time you will have started up and taxied out on one tank; now is the time to prove the other. So select the other main tank and begin the run-up as follows:

1. Open the throttle to the recommended RPM for propeller exercise (when a constant speed airscrew is fitted). This is usually done at 2000 to 2200 RPM. Move back the RPM lever taking care not to go into the feathering gate (when there is one). Look for a drop in engine speed, then move the lever back to the fully fine position. Repeat that twice to exercise the propeller and warm up the oil.

2. Reduce power to that recommended for the magneto checks (usually between 1700 and 2000 RPM). Switch to the LEFT magneto, check that the RPM drop does not exceed the maximum permitted (usually 150 RPM but sometimes more). Return the switch to BOTH then select RIGHT magneto, note the decrease in RPM and ensure that it does not differ from the other magneto by more than the permitted amount (usually 50 RPM). Return the switch to BOTH. The ignition is now checked for that engine.

3. In aircraft with fuel injected engines select ALTERNATE AIR to see that it is functioning. In the case of carburettor engines select HOT air and, if one is fitted, note the rise in temperature on the Carb. Air Temperature Gauge. There should also be a decrease in RPM. Return the selector to COLD and the reverse indications should occur.

4. Check instrument vacuum (or pressure in some aircraft systems) and electric charge. Check oil pressure and be alert for any unusual sounds or vibration.

5. Throttle back to 1500 RPM. Bring the pitch lever back to the feather gate (when applicable) and leave it there to check that there is no change in RPM. If there is, the CSU (Constant Speed Unit) is faulty. Move the pitch lever into FEATHER but be prepared to go back into the normal operating range as soon as a drop in RPM is indicated. On no account allow the RPM to go below 1000.

6. Close the throttle fully and note the slow running RPM which

should be normal for the engine (see manual), then open the throttle to idling speed which is usually 1000–1200 RPM. At that setting:

    a) The alternator/generator will sustain the electric load;
    b) The plugs should not foul up;
    c) The temperature of the engine should remain within limits.

7.   If you are flying a twin now check the other engine.

Should you, at any time, forget to change tanks prior to the power checks on no account do so afterwards and immediately before take-off because, if there is a fuel line blockage, that is when you will find out!

   Now, and only now, may you call up for take-off clearance and make that flight to Funfield. The various checks can be thoroughly completed in less time than it takes to read these pages. And they are worth every second in terms of safety.

3. OPERATING FROM AIRSTRIPS AND PRIVATE FIELDS

The day comes when the student pilot gains his new PPL or CPL and for the first time he is more or less a free agent. Now he can take his family and friends for a fly around and spread his wings. Pilots who have to hire an aircraft from the local club or school are, to some extent, subject to the eagle eye of a flying instructor, but those who are able to buy their own light 'plane have a degree of freedom that brings out the best in some – and the worst in others. Because those blessed with private wings of their own can operate without reference to an experienced pilot, they have the freedom (provided they remain within the law) to do all manner of things which can easily put them at risk. For there is no short cut to experience. It is only gained in one way – over the years and in hours spent flying.

It will only be a matter of time before our new pilot receives a 'come-visit-me' invitation from some friendly farmer with a big field or perhaps friends who live near a private airstrip. Sad to relate, the accident statistics are knee deep in landing and take-off incidents at such fields, and it is not only the inexperienced pilots who make the mistakes, but also those with plenty of time in their log books. One can make excuses for the inexperienced but no pilot need get himself in at the deep end just because the landing or take-off is not at an international-size airport.

Why do small airfield or airstrip operations cause so many accidents? In the main because pilots have little knowledge of:

1.   Field performance and how it is affected by various conditions.

2.   Short take-off and landing techniques.

3.   Correct use of flap.

Aircraft performance

In the UK an interesting analysis was made of take-off and landing accidents. It was found that in 85 per cent of the take-off incidents wind strength was less than 15 knots. 55 per cent occurred while taking off from private strips and 65 per cent happened when the field was less than 1650ft (500m) long. 70 per cent of the landing accidents happened when there was less than a 10 knot wind, 80 per cent were on wet grass, 55 per cent of the accidents were in fields offering less than 1650ft of landing run and in 60 per cent of the cases mentioned first touchdown was made quarter to half way into the field.

What do these statistics reveal? Well, part of the trouble is that many pilots do not make proper use of the Owners/Operators/Flight Manual. Why should they? After all the place where they trained for a licence probably had runways that went on forever and disappeared over the horizon. So when he does visit that airstrip, it will probably be the first time he has had to ask if it is big enough. Sometimes the length of run available for take-off and landing is published but sometimes it is not and we are left to rely on word of mouth. Possibly the owner of the field or a pilot who has landed there will come up with 'it's about 500 metres long' or 'there's room for a 707'. 500m or 1650ft, is the figure so often mentioned in performance accident statistics. And it is a long held belief by many pilots, an aviation myth if you like, that 500m is the magic figure and if you have 500m at your disposal *any* light single will take off or land without drama. Unfortunately like many myths this one is not true. The facts are best illustrated by examining the take-off requirements for a well known light aircraft being flown by the thousand in most parts of the world. Take-off run (i.e. ground roll, as opposed to take-off distance which relates to a position where the aircraft has gained a height of 50ft (15m) above airfield level) is quoted as 780ft (240m), comfortably within that 1650ft so often believed to be adequate. However, 780ft is conditional on the following:

1. A sea-level airfield.

2. A hard, level runway.

3. ISA conditions (i.e. temperature is + 15°C or 59°F).

4. Still air.

5. Aircraft at maximum weight but in 'as new' condition.

Under these circumstances the aircraft can be operated safely into and out of a 1650ft field provided, of course, there are no high trees or power lines on the approach or in the flight path immediately after crossing the hedge following take-off. The problems start when pilots make no allowance for the variables. And each of the following variables can have a profound effect on that 780ft (240m).

1. A tailwind component amounting to 10 per cent of aircraft lift-off speed (say, 6 knots for the average light single) will add 20 per cent to the take-off run.

2. A 10 per cent increase in weight will add 20 per cent to the length of take-off run.

3. An increase of 10°C (20°F) in temperature above ISA will add 20 per cent to the take-off run.

4. You must allow a 10 per cent increase in take-off run for each 1000ft airfield elevation above sea level.

5. Long grass or soft ground can add 25 per cent to the take-off run and may in extreme cases prevent you from getting airborne.

6. An uphill slope of only 2 degrees will add 10 per cent to the take-off run.

The cumulative effect of these variables amounts to this: when a pilot attempts a take-off in his slightly overweight aircraft when the strip is 1650ft (500m) long with a gentle incline, the grass has not been cut for weeks, the field is 2000ft (600m) amsl and tall trees at one end make it necessary for him to accept a modest tailwind, the normal 780ft (240m) take-off run (at sea level) becomes extended to 2460ft (614m). But it does not end here; all performances quoted in the aircraft's manual assume that the airplane is in good condition and the engine is giving its full power. When the elastic is a little past its prime that 2460ft could become even longer. The situation so far described is illustrated in Fig. 6 and, on the basis that prevention is always better than cure, here are some hints aimed at preventing performance accidents, particularly as they apply to operating out of small fields.

The take-off

Use of flap

Yet another deeply entrenched belief, worshipped by some pilots almost as though it were a religious rite, is that use of flap will improve the take-off performance of any aircraft. It is true that flap must be used in high performance aircraft – otherwise the journey would continue by road! But these aircraft, as a result of carrying the maximum load on the smallest possible wing in order to minimize drag, have very high stalling speeds. The flaps on such aircraft, which may be double or treble Fowler devices allied to leading edge flaps of the Kruger type, reduce the stalling speed by 60 knots or more. On the other hand, most of the modern light singles and twins are equipped with slotted flaps – anaemic gadgets that take no more than 6 to 12 knots off the stalling speed. This is hardly surprising in view of the low speeds involved. Nonetheless, some quite experienced pilots, among them flying instructors, feel it their duty to copy airline practice, even when the equipment at their disposal bears little resemblance

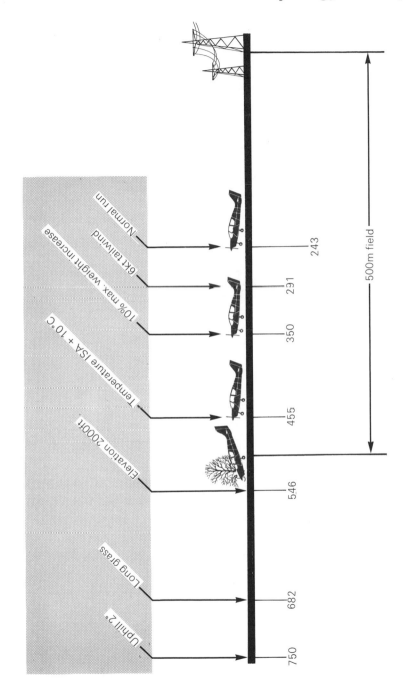

Fig. 6: Cumulative effect of anti-take-off factors.

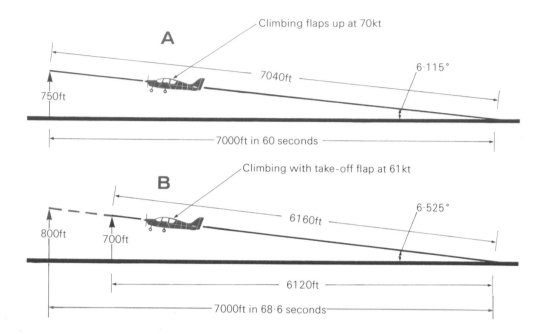

Fig. 7: To flap or not to flap? Aircraft B is climbing with take-off flap at a slightly lower than flaps-up speed. Since climb rate is only slightly reduced there is a marginal improvement in climb gradient of less than 0.5 degree. That is the theory — it does not work with all aircraft.

to a fast public transport jet. That can be counter-productive and even dangerous.

The reasoning behind use of flap for take-off is based on the premise that almost the same rate of climb as that achieved flaps-up may be maintained at a lower forward speed when take-off flap is selected. Fig. 7 shows that, when it works, take-off flap can make a small but useful improvement to climb gradient compared with a flap-up departure. Unfortunately it does not work with all aircraft for although rate of climb is dependent upon surplus horsepower, angle of climb is a function of surplus thrust. And that is a different ball game because thrust is affected by things other than the power being fed to the propeller, e.g. blade angle relative to propeller airflow (which is likewise affected by engine RPM), forward speed and whether or not there is a constant speed propeller.

By now it will be realized that the variables involved make this a complicated subject, even before we consider type of flap and the effects of wind. The simple answer is that you should consult the aircraft manual. If it says 'no flap' then leave them alone.

If flap is recommended it is essential to use the correct climbing speed for this configuration because there is no point whatsoever in lowering, say, 10 to 15 degrees and then using the flaps-up speed. When flap is used on aircraft not designed for the technique the most likely result will be a reduction in climb gradient.

Assessing the available take-off run

Properly established airstrips usually have published information concerning field elevation, obstructions and length of landing or take-off areas. It is when you are about to leap into the air from an ordinary field that special problems arise because even the owner of the land may have no accurate idea of the distance from one hedge to the other.

There are those among us who would claim among their special talents the ability to gaze at the far end of the field and announce with conviction 'she will sail out of here'. This has been known to precede 'did you spot my deliberate mistake?' a question usually asked as the pilot extracts himself from a heap of bent aircraft residing in the next field. It should be remembered that all manner of features can distort scale and give a totally optimistic impression of distance. And the final moments of preparing for a take-off out of an unknown field are not the time for optimism.

The obvious method of assessing the length of a field is to pace it out. The walk will do you good and the surface can be inspected at close quarters (if you have the misfortune to fall down a hole and break your leg, take my advice – don't attempt the take-off). Most males believe their average step to be about 3ft (1m) in length, but with the majority of folk it is considerably less and, in fact, nearer 30in (0.75m). So 500 paces would represent about 416yd (380m) instead of the imagined 500, i.e. 17 per cent less take-off distance than you might believe. As an insurance for the future try walking normally over a measured distance, count the paces and thus determine the length of your stride. This boy-scout-type information may be of value to you one day.

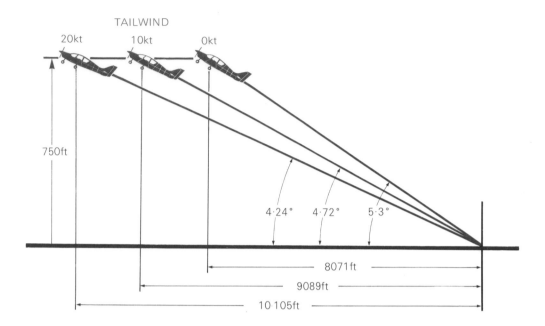

Fig. 8: Effect of tailwind on climb gradient (in the interests of clarity, height is shown at a larger scale than distance in this illustration).

Assessing the surface

The rolling friction caused by soft ground and long grass can, as already mentioned, prevent you from reaching take-off speed in the available distance. So when the surface inspection gives you cause for concern, try a take-off without passengers before attempting one at higher weight. But if the aircraft refuses to accelerate abandon the take-off while there is room ahead, bearing in mind that if the grass is wet your brakes will be less effective than usual.

Selecting take-off direction

Tall trees, power lines etc. at one end of the field leave you with little choice in selecting take-off direction and this may mean you have to accept a tailwind component. Furthermore there may be other obstacles to clear that are situated some distance from the field, and a gentle avoiding turn more or less immediately after lift-off might be necessary. Assessing climb path under these circumstances is not a task for the inexperienced, but Fig. 8 will at least illustrate the effects of a 10 knot and a 20 knot tailwind on climb gradient.

Without doubt when the surface wind exceeds 10 knots it must be regarded as the predominant factor and a downwind take-off should be avoided at all costs, even when the field is quite large.

Estimating wind speed and direction

Taking the easier part first, wind direction may be determined when there is enough breeze to flutter a handkerchief or blow away a fistful of grass that has been thrown into the air. Another method is to watch cloud movements, remembering that at 1500ft the wind veers through 15 degrees so allow for that when using clouds in the sky or their shadows on the ground.

Light and variable winds are a trap because tailwinds can appear from nowhere. So whenever possible pick the longest run, with the fewest obstructions for the take-off.

Assessing wind strength is the main problem. All manner of 'ancient mariner' type advice is on record and I have picked the best available (see table on page 48).

Take-off technique – short field

Away from the discipline of an airfield there is a temptation to avoid the pre-take-off checks and this must at all costs be resisted because at no time are they more important than when operating out of a small field. The walk-around must be completed with care (see page 33) and everything has to be on the top line.

When there is snow or mud on the field, taxi to the holding point then get out of the aircraft and have a quick look at the wheel spats (when fitted). If these have filled with mud or snow on the way out this could prevent take-off even from the biggest of runways.

Go through the power checks in the normal way, then line up at the beginning of the run. If the strip is very short push the tail back to the far boundary – that little trick once saved my neck while flying out of a disused football pitch surrounded by an unbelievably solid stone wall.

Beaufort Scale	Description	Average Speed (knots)	Symptoms (over land areas)
0	Calm	0	Smoke rises vertically
1	Light air	2	Smoke, but not wind vanes, indicate direction
2	Light breeze	5	Wind felt on face; leaves rustle; vanes moved by wind
3	Gentle breeze	9	Leaves and small twigs in constant motion; small flags extend
4	Moderate breeze	14	Raises dust and loose paper; moves small branches
5	Fresh breeze	19	Small trees in leaf begin to sway; crested wavelets on lakes
6	Strong breeze	24	Large branches in motion; telegraph wires whistle
7	Moderate gale	30	Whole trees in motion; effort required to walk against wind
8	Fresh gale	37	Breaks twigs off trees; generally impedes progress
9	Strong gale	44	Slight damage to buildings (slates and chimney pots removed)

The numbers go up to force 12 (Hurricane) but you should not be flying out of small fields when the wind exceeds force 6 or 7 unless you have a lot of experience in this kind of operation.

If the manual says use flaps for a short take-off then use them, lift off at the recommended speed and climb at the correct flaps-down speed. Be quite clear about these speeds – they can make or break the exercise. Avoid at all costs any so-called expert theories which have little fact to back them up. An example of one of these is the practice of lowering flap while accelerating before lift-off. Better by far to concentrate on keeping straight and rotating at the correct speed.

When clear to take off, open up power on the brakes, remind yourself of the lift-off and climb-out speeds, then let her go. As soon as direction is established ease back on the control yoke to remove the load from the nosewheel. Check the engine instruments and if it all looks good continue with the take-off. On the other hand low RPM or any other abnormal indications, such as vibration or rough running are all an invitation to abandon the take-off. You must, however, make the decision while there is sufficient room ahead in which to stop.

At the correct speed, lift the aircraft off the ground and allow the air-speed to build up naturally until the correct IAS appears. When flap has been used it is vital to adopt the correct speed for the climb. Remember the only way flaps can improve the climb gradient is if a near normal rate of climb can be maintained at a lower than usual forward speed.

Take-off technique – soft field

When the problems of taking off from a short field are compounded by soft ground conditions (i.e. mud or snow) the normal take-off technique previously described could prove inadequate and, since failing to clear the far hedge is an expensive way to find this out, it is better in these conditions to adopt the proper soft field technique.

All the preliminaries already described apply up to the point where power is applied against the brakes. However, in the soft field technique the control yoke is held fully back. Drastic as this may sound it works well, the reasoning being as follows. As the aircraft accelerates, most of the load is removed from the nosewheel so that it does not have to behave like a plough, absorbing engine power in the process. When the airflow is sufficient to activate the elevators the wings will be ready to fly. So the sequence of events is to apply full power and release the brakes with the control wheel fully back. The aircraft accelerates until the elevators take effect, the nose comes up, the angle of attack increases and the wings take a bite on the air, lifting the aircraft and its happy, relieved inmates.

A word of warning here. In a well regulated situation when the nose comes up the tail should also go down, and in some aircraft there is a tendency for the tail bumper to touch the ground. So be prepared; as the elevators take effect, relax a little of the backward pressure off the control yoke and allow the aircraft to lift off in an attitude which, if rather more nose-up than usual, at least does not threaten to launch you into outer space.

The landing

The problem with landing on a private strip or field, as opposed to taking off is that it is usually not possible to pace out the available run before the event. So unless the intended landing area is an established one with published information we are back to the owner's assurance of 'yes, you can get in alright'. The trouble is that field owners, and some pilots, have been known to express such reassuring views without considering the other part of the deal – will it fly out again?.

At the beginning of this chapter I quoted some accident statistics, among them the fact that 60 per cent of the landing accidents featured a first touchdown that was quarter to half way into the field. Hang around your local airfield one day and watch the light aircraft coming in to land. I would be surprised if you did not find the following:

1. Many pilots cross the airfield boundary too high and too fast.

2. Some of these pilots use only part flap.

3. As a result of these two mistakes many pilots touch down too far along the runway.

4. In most cases the nosewheel touches down simultaneously with the main landing gear.

If they come in like express trains on a proper airfield it is hardly surprising that so many pilots, some of them quite experienced, come to grief while trying to land among the cows. Before talking of procedures it might be of value to discuss one of the most misunderstood controls on the aircraft – flaps.

The function of flaps

It is a strange anomaly of aviation life that many pilots insist on using flap for take-off, even in instances when it has no beneficial effect on the aircraft type, the runway will take a Jumbo Jet and there is a 20 knot wind blowing. Yet, for a reason I have never been able to discover, these same pilots have an aversion to using full flap while landing.

Whatever their design, flaps are intended to provide two aerodynamic functions:

1. A decrease in stalling speed made possible by an increase in lift.

2. An increase in drag which may be used to the pilot's benefit.

While flaps differ in design concept, one can generalize and say that the main lift increase comes from the first 15 to 25 degrees of their depression. Further lowering of flap causes a small additional increase in lift but the main effect of this part of the movement is a marked increase in drag. This is illustrated in Fig. 9 (see next page).

The most commonly used flaps on small aircraft are of the slotted type which open up a small gap between their own leading edge and the wing shroud. While such devices are moderately successful in increasing the lift coefficient of the wing, they do a pretty poor job at increasing drag. Blame this on fashion. There was a time when designers almost universally fitted split flaps, which were practically as good at increasing lift as slotted flaps, probably simpler to manufacture, and infinitely better when it came to producing more drag. Even the best flaps, like the area-increasing Fowler devices, can only reduce the stalling speed by a percentage of the basic, flaps-up figure. And when that figure is relatively low, as it would be in the case of most light singles, it follows that the decrease must be low. Some types of flap are illustrated in Fig. 10 (page 53).

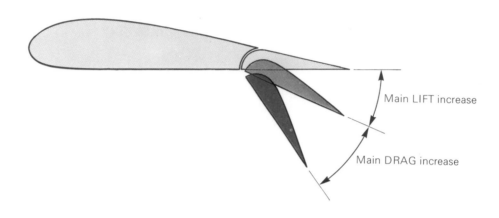

Fig. 9: Main lift increase with most flaps comes during the first 15 to 25 degrees of depression. Further flap application causes a modest lift increase and a significant build-up in drag.

With most (but not all) light aircraft flaps can only produce a modest decrease in stalling speed. Consequently their main value is their ability to produce drag on the approach, so enabling the pilot to control his descent path with precision and arrive at a pre-determined touchdown point. Yet this is the very talent of flaps that so many pilots seem reluctant to use.

Misuse of flap

While a refusal to use full flap is one widespread handling fault among pilots, another common error is a passion to bang on the lot in one go, usually on the base leg. The correct procedure is to apply part flap, say half, on base leg and leave the application of full flap until short finals. In that way you will avoid staggering in against what may be a strong

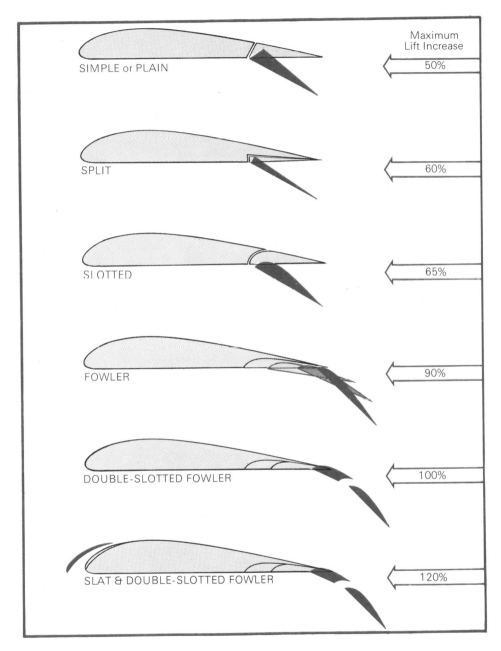

Fig. 10: Types of flap in common use.

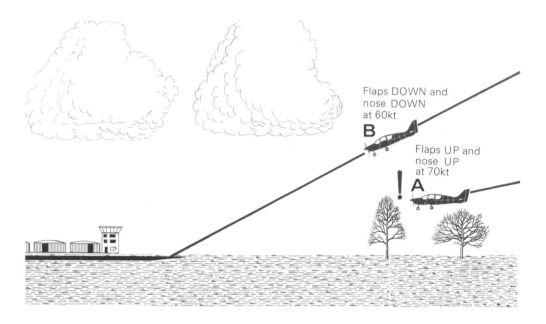

Flaps DOWN and
nose DOWN
at 60kt

B

Flaps UP and
nose UP
at 70kt

! **A**

Fig.11: Dangers of a flat approach, the result of using only part flap.

headwind. Nevertheless, strong wind or not, full flap must be applied on short finals when you are committed to the landing because only in this configuration are you assured of the best transition from air to ground. The only exception to the full flap rule is in conditions of crosswind when most aircraft handle better with half flap. For advice on crosswind flap settings consult the aircraft manual.

Failure to use the flaps properly is sometimes compounded by adopting too high an approach speed. In fact many pilots have a tendency to use the best glide speed (i.e. best Lift/Drag Ratio Speed) and this is bound to result in a rather flat approach with little scope for adjusting the rate of descent with the throttles. Take a look at Fig. 11. The pilot in aircraft A is approaching at the flaps-up best gliding speed of 70 knots. The nose is high, obscuring the view ahead and, since the glide path is flat even when the throttle is fully closed, obstacle clearance is very poor. There is every chance that he will hang it in the trees before reaching the runway.

Pilot B on the other hand is coming in at 60 knots, a speed somewhat lower than that for best L/D so he can control his descent rate (and therefore glide path) by adjusting the throttle. Furthermore, he has lowered some flap and although his speed is 10 knots below that of Pilot A the nose is lower and he can see where he is going. Finally, because of the steeper and more controllable descent path, obstacle clearance is better. And the additional drag generated by the flaps means that more power must be used to obtain the required flight path, slipstream is increased and the rudder and elevators are more effective.

Selecting the landing path

When landing at an established airstrip you will probably have published information to guide you and your arrival will be quite straightforward, although naturally you will have to take extra care as private strips, even those with published details, are usually very much smaller than public airfields.

The small strip or private field which has no published details is another matter, and in selecting the landing path at one of these you must bear in mind:

1. Wind direction.

2. Crosswind limits for the aircraft.

3. Obstructions on the approach.

4. Obstructions in the overshoot area.

5. Available landing run.

6. Whether to land uphill and downwind or the other way round when there is an incline.

By now it will be apparent that operating into and out of small fields is a skilled business.

On the basis of being sure rather than sorry it is a good idea to fly a dummy run over the field (to the right of the intended landing path so that you can check the approaches by looking out to the left). This should be conducted at a safe height, checking for tall trees, power lines etc. while at the same time assessing turbulence, wind direction and the size of the field.

Method of approach

Go further downwind than for a normal approach so that you will have a good straight run into the field, allowing yourself plenty of time to become established at the right speed and on the correct descent path.

On base leg lower half flap, reduce speed to that recommended for an engine-assisted approach, add a little power to control the rate of descent and re-trim. Make a gradual turn on to landing strip centreline and, as you approach the field, lower full flap (unless there is a crosswind). Reduce speed by another 5 or 10 knots according to aircraft type and select a touchdown point just inside the field boundary.

On the approach, aim to come in on a descending path, keeping the selected touchdown point fixed in relation to the windscreen area by using the following methods of correction:

a) Overshooting: Landing point moving down the windscreen and field standing on end.
Remedy: *Reduce* power and lower the nose slightly.

b) Undershooting: Landing point moving up the windscreen and field becoming flatter.
Remedy: *Increase* power and raise the nose slightly.

Although the 'creeper' method of approach used to be favoured a descending path is certainly better when you have to cross a hedge or other boundary. This is illustrated in Fig. 12. Whatever technique you use it is essential that the aircraft is flown at a lower approach speed than usual so that it is on the 'back of the drag curve', i.e. power is needed to limit the rate of descent.

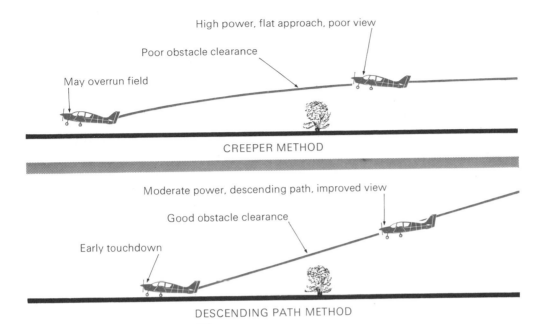

Fig. 12: The short field approach. The creeper method is rarely warranted as this illustration will show.

Guard against drifting into a 'high power, nose up' situation as this restricts the view ahead. In fact a long, low drag of this kind invariably makes you land too far down the field. This is illustrated in the upper drawing of Fig. 12.

The landing

Having crossed the field boundary at a lower airspeed than usual, allow the aircraft to descend near the ground. Then, shortly before the selected touchdown point, complete the round-out and then close the throttle. As a result of its low airspeed, the aircraft should land almost immediately. The arrival should be on the mainwheels only. *On no account close the throttle until immediately before touchdown,* otherwise the bird will sink like a winged brick.

The low-speed short landing demands skill and, as with any other task requiring expertise, the only way to become proficient is through practice.

Go up to a safe height, lower full flap, add a little power and see how slowly you can fly. With practice you can pull off some astonishingly short landings, but delay reducing to your minimum arrival speed until full flap has been applied and you are on short finals.

Use of brake

Under normal circumstances you can apply the brakes fairly decisively as soon as the nosewheel has made contact with the ground, but beware if the grass is wet, as the wheels can sometimes lock and, unless the touchdown is near the downwind boundary, the aircraft will most likely skid into the far hedge. During the post-landing run it is good practice to safeguard the nosewheel by holding the control yoke fully back.

Operating into and out of small strips is a demanding exercise but provided the principles outlined in this chapter are strictly followed there need be no drama.

4. A WORD ABOUT INSTRUMENT FLYING

'I start on the usual compass course with a mentally calculated allowance for drift which I shall correct on a known landmark ten miles hence; but after six miles I find there are tree-covered hills, shrouded in wisps of cloud . . . the ground is gradually rising to the hills south of Beauvais and the clouds become slightly lower. Visibility has decreased to some 500 yards – I fly about 150 feet from the ground – am compelled to stick to this road as completely as a motor-car for if I lose sight of it I am to all intents lost.' Thus wrote the pioneer British airline pilot, Frank Courtney, of his experiences while flying the London–Paris route in 1924.

Wireless, as it was then known, offered morse communications on an 'if you are lucky' basis and the only gyro instrument was a crude affair driven by a little propeller which at the time was as advanced to pilots like Courtney as the modern Flight Director System is today.

'Flying by instruments,' Courtney continued, 'for say 200 miles, is a new form of flying, so I strongly contend that all commercial pilots should be given plenty of practice in this blind flying when not engaged in ordinary flying' – shades of the Instrument Rating and things to come!

Clearly a situation in which the fare-paying customers were expected to relax in their wicker chairs while a leather-clad, hairy pilot pressed on under a lowering cloudbase was one that could not be allowed to continue.

Two well-equipped offices, Cessna Citation 1 above and British Aerospace 125/700 below. The facilities offered by these outstanding flight decks can be of full value only to the pilot who understands exactly how best to use what is before him.

So the 1930s saw the widespread introduction of gyro instruments in the form of good Turn and Slip indicators, direction indicators and various attitude indicating instruments which were finally standardized in the Artificial Horizon. It was not long before even quite small aircraft were being fitted with these instruments which enabled a pilot to control attitude, heading and, through the pressure instruments, height and performances without visual reference to the ground. They did not, and indeed to this day cannot, tell a pilot where he is in relation to a position on the ground. That special talent had to wait until radio technology caught up with airframes and engines (and their ability to lose a pilot at high speed).

Most readers of this book will at some time in their training have received formal instruction in basic instrument flying while those with an instrument rating will have learned much more. For it is one thing to fly on instruments and quite another to do so while trying to follow verbal or radio instrument instructions. To the instrument-qualified reader much of this chapter will be last year's news. However, it should help those who have, at some time past, had a little instrument instruction and found out the rest for themselves.

In essence do-it-yourself instrument flying is about as desirable as do-it-yourself brain surgery. In fact brief details of the accidents that have resulted from non-instrument pilots pressing on into deteriorating weather would fill many books. That pilots without instrument flying skills do fly into weather that is probably beyond not only their own capability but also that of the aircraft is an established fact. Why they do it is not so clear. The human factors listed on pages 14 and 16 no doubt contribute but the following are weaknesses which have particular relevance to accidents which result from attempts to continue flying into IMC.

1. Lack of clear understanding of how to obtain the best results from the flight instruments.

2. Failure to appreciate how information from the radio navigation aids should be related to the flight instruments.

3. Lack of the necessary instrument flying skill to make use of the information.

Functions and techniques of instrument flying

Before any attempt is made at serious instrument navigation the pilot must be clear about the function of the equipment in his aircraft and how the various instruments interrelate. When the weather becomes hostile and outside visual references are lost the pilot is faced with the following tasks.

1. He must fly the aircraft safely at a required Flight Level, Altitude or Height and on a prescribed heading. This is achieved with reference to the flight panel which is made up of gyro and pressure instruments.

2. He must guide the aircraft in a direction certain to avoid high terrain, other air traffic and restricted areas and at the destination he will have to descend down a glide path in line with the runway. While the various headings, heights, rates of climb/descent and speeds are flown on the flight panel, using basic instrument flying skills, the information needed to attain the correct flight path is obtained from a radar controller or with reference to the radio instruments (VOR/ILS/ADF etc.).

Although these may sound obvious and somewhat academic points they are nevertheless worth stressing because so often one sees pilots steering on the Radio Compass. Some even try it on the VOR although these two radio instruments are there to tell the pilot where he is in relation to a ground facility. They do not provide heading information.

For the various holding patterns, joining procedures and approaches to be flown a pilot must be capable of changing radio frequencies, setting up equipment, locating the correct approach charts and complying with ATC instructions – all this, and more, while flying on instruments. It is a job fit for a one-armed paper hanger and by now it will be clear that the building blocks of accurate radio navigation have good basic instrument flying as a main ingredient. And since many of the instrument rating trappers name indifferent instrument flying as the main cause of failure during test a little paper revision may be of value.

The name of the game is *relax*. A pilot who grips the controls like a vice, knuckles gleaming white, is in no position to fly accurately, certainly not in a light aircraft. Of course one can only relax when one is not afraid of the unexpected and is in the right attitude of mind. For instrument flying is not some form of emergency; to those who earn a living in the sharp end of the ship this type of aviation is more the rule than the exception. So back to basics.

Reading the instrument panel

There was a time when the instruments were arranged to fill up odd holes in the instrument panel. One could fly an aircraft on one day in which the Turn and Slip indicator was below the Artificial Horizon, and the next day fly another type of 'plane and find it in a quite different position. The first serious attempt at designing a standard flight panel which would enjoy widespread use was probably that devised by the UK Royal Air Force. After the Second World War it was modified slightly to become the internationally accepted Basic 'T'. The advantages of a standard panel may be likened to the charms of having a standard typewriter keyboard. Think of the chaos that would result among typists if each manufacturer laid out the letters in a different order. Likewise the Basic 'T' enables a pilot to learn by heart what, for example, a Rate 1 turn to the left should look like, so that when he makes the transition on to another aircraft type his past experience should stand him in good stead.

Various methods of reading the instrument panel have been championed, among them the total concept (where the entire panel is read like a word in one lump as opposed to piece by piece) and Selective Radial Scan. While I have in the past rather liked the total concept, Selective Radial Scan seems to be the most generally accepted and, since most flying training authorities throughout the world support it, this is the method I shall describe.

The idea behind Selective Radial Scan is that for each manoeuvre on instruments one assesses attitude on the Artificial Horizon, cross-referencing its indications by moving the eyes back and forth in turn to the others directly involved (Fig. 13). For example in a descent it would work this way:

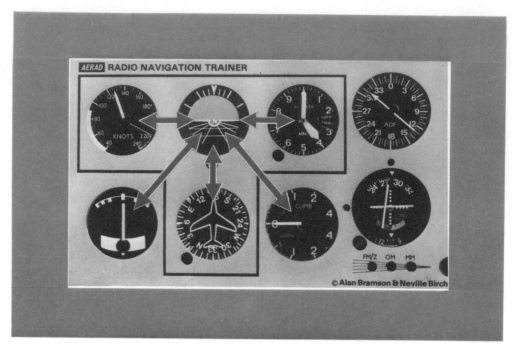

Fig. 13: Selective Radial Scan.

1. Reduce power to achieve the required rate of descent.

2. Check wings are level on the Artificial Horizon and adopt the descent attitude. Re-trim.

3. Check the ASI for correct speed then go back to the AH.

4. Check heading on the DI (known as a DG in the USA) then go back to the AH.

5. Check rate of descent on the VSI. Assuming the airspeed is correct, if the rate of descent is too slow reduce power and lower the nose slightly, and if it is too fast increase power and raise the nose slightly. Go back to the AH.

6. Check your descent progress on the altimeter, then go back to the AH.

7. Continue moving the eyes between the AH, VSI, DI and occasion-
    ally the ball (to check balance). As the altimeter comes within 50ft
    of the required level add power, adopt the cruising attitude on the
    AH and re-trim.

Note that the scan moves radially between the attitude instrument and the
others involved. In this case balance is only occasionally scanned. During
other manoeuvres some instruments become more important than others
and the scan is varied accordingly.

Flying the basic manoeuvres on instruments

Descending has been used to illustrate Selective Radial Scan, and climbing
is very similar with two provisos:

1. More attention will have to be devoted to heading and balance
    while under climbing power.

2. At the required flight level climbing power should be left on until
    after the cruising attitude has been established. Then as the ASI
    approaches cruising speed the power can be adjusted.

Maintaining straight and level flight (Fig. 14)

Having established cruising attitude on the Artificial Horizon and trimmed
for the condition, fine adjustments in pitch should be made using the ASI.
Continue the scan, bringing in the VSI and altimeter to ensure that the
aircraft is neither climbing nor descending at the required airspeed. If you
want to fly at a specific power setting, for example, 65 per cent, then let the
airspeed settle to a figure that maintains a steady flight level. When a
particular airspeed is required then power adjustments will be needed to
prevent a climb or descent.

The most common fault among inexperienced instrument pilots is
failure to maintain the required heading, usually because it is often not

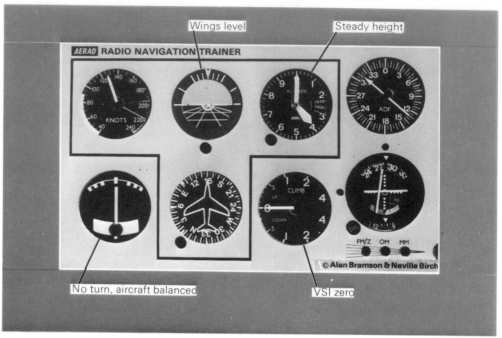

Fig. 14: Straight and level flight.

realized how little bank is required to provoke a turn; a few degrees roll, left or right, will start that DI on its way.

Finally, like any steady mode of flight, accurate trim is all-important while flying straight and level on instruments.

As far as climbing, descending and cruising flight are concerned it should be remembered that:

$$\textbf{power} + \textbf{attitude} = \textbf{performance}$$

and while most pilots automatically accept this during visual flight it is sometimes forgotten while flying on the clocks. In other words if you want a particular rate of climb, rate of descent or cruising speed, all matters that are indicated on the performance instruments (i.e. ASI, VSI) the correct attitude must be adopted and held with reference to the Artificial Horizon and the right amount of power must be applied.

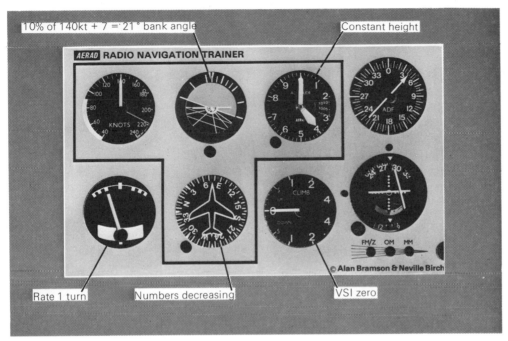

Fig. 15: The Rate 1 turn (to the left).

Turning (Fig. 15)

Since rate of turn is a function of airspeed and angle of bank it is convenient to know what angle to adopt on the Artificial Horizon. The Rate 1 turn is the standard used for instrument procedures and it is a simple matter to find the angle of bank:

$$10\% \text{ of the IAS in knots } +7$$
$$\text{or}$$
$$10\% \text{ of the IAS in mph } +5$$

So at 130 knots the bank angle would be $13 + 7 = 20$ degrees and so forth. Provided the bank angle is maintained the turn should proceed at approximately Rate 1, but when higher levels of accuracy are demanded the watch must be used, allowing 30 degrees of heading change every ten seconds.

While turning, the scan should take in the VSI and altimeter to ensure that altitude is being maintained, the DI should be checked for progress

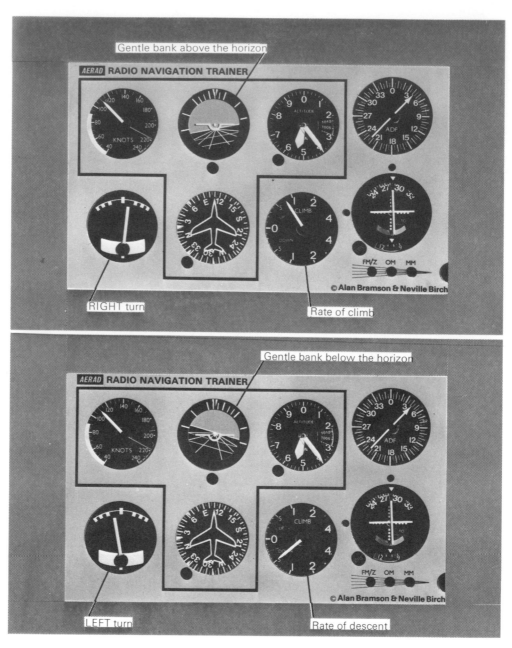

Fig. 16: Climbing and descending turns.

(rolling out of the turn some 10 degrees before reaching the new heading) and the ball should be in balance. There will be a small decrease in airspeed during the turn but this you can blame on the laws of aerodynamics and ignore.

Climbing and descending turns (Fig. 16)

When you want to make a climbing turn while maintaining a high rate of ascent you should apply maximum climbing power and attain the appropriate climbing speed. Since wing loading, and therefore power requirement, increase with angle of bank it follows that when climb rate is important angle of bank must be restricted – in fact to the point where a Rate 1 turn is achieved and no more.

It is common operating practice to forsake the best-rate-of-climb technique, which along with circuits and bumps formed part of training school days, and go for a cruise-climb. This method, while sacrificing feet per minute, has the advantage that you cover more miles along the route while attaining cruising level. From the instrument flying point of view the only trap is the aircraft's natural desire to overbank while in a climbing turn. Conversely, during a descending turn there is a tendency to underbank. You must in both cases take care to maintain a constant bank angle with reference to the Artificial Horizon.

Since rates of climb and descent are closely related to power used at any particular airspeed it is useful to know the approximate manifold pressure and RPM for the conditions of flight, remembering to adjust the throttle and hold the pressure constant as the aircraft climbs or descends.

Flight on the limited panel

While it is comforting to remind oneself that Artificial Horizons hardly ever give trouble these days, it nevertheless can happen. That is why it is common practice to fit a Turn and Slip indicator which is driven off a different system from that for the other gyro instrument.

Imagine you did lose the Artificial Horizon at night or in cloud. Could you cope on the remaining instruments without raising the blood pressure?

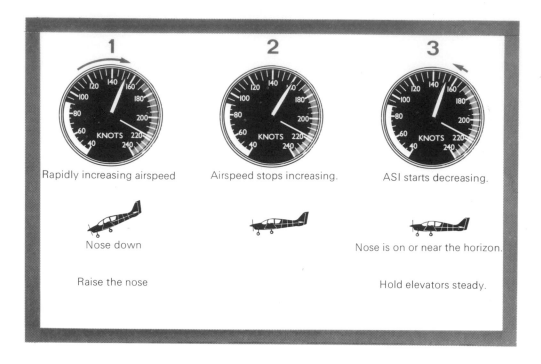

Fig. 17: Recovery from a steep, nose-down attitude on the limited panel.

And suppose you got yourself into a stall/spin situation – can you place hand on heart and say 'yes, I could recover'?

In my experience few pilots know how to recover from an extreme nose-up or nose-down attitude on the basic panel, let alone stalls or spins, and since the first two are problems you are more likely to have to tackle, here is the procedure to adopt. Unlike some methods being canvassed, one or two of them calling for pilots with two left hands and a couple of rights, the correct way is very simple.

Recovery from a dive (Fig. 17)

You are flying along, minding your own business, when without warning the airspeed begins to increase very rapidly, the turn needle and ball are in the centre. Being no fool (and of a quick disposition) you tell yourself 'I am in a dive'. To recover:

1.　Leave the throttle alone but ease back on the control yoke.

2.　Continue progressive, *gentle* back pressure until the airspeed stops increasing.

3.　Watch the ASI. The needle will now start to move back towards the original cruising speed. At that point the nose is on or near the horizon, so –

4.　Hold the stick in its present position, allow the airspeed to increase and if necessary assist the process with slight forward pressure on the control yoke.

5.　Check the trim and if necessary adjust it when the aircraft has settled at the correct airspeed.

While recovery from the dive is in progress use the ailerons to keep the turn needle centred and maintain balance using the rudder in response to ball displacement (i.e. ball to the left – correct with left rudder. Ball to the right – correct with right rudder).

Recovery from a steep, nose-high attitude (Fig. 18)

This situation is very similar to the dive recovery already explained except that the initial indication will be a rapidly decreasing airspeed which threatens to go 'off the clock'. Recovery is simply a matter of applying forward pressure on the control yoke until the decrease is arrested. Then when the ASI needle starts to move back towards the original speed the nose is on or near the horizon and you should complete the recovery as described for the dive.

Spins and spiral dives (Fig. 19)

The difference in instrument indications between these two nasties is illustrated in Fig. 19. Although when viewed from the ground or seen as instrument indications there would appear to be similarities between these two manoeuvres they are in fact quite different. In the spin the air-speed is low, usually fluctuating around stalling speed, and there will probably be some outward skid. On the other hand spiral dives, which are

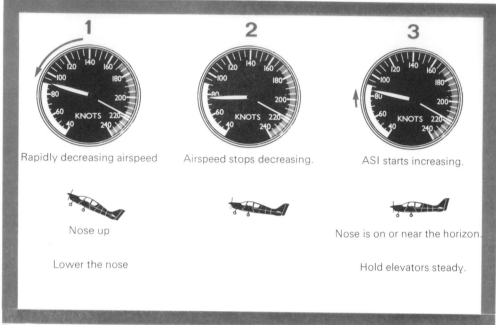

Fig. 18: Recovery from a steep, nose-up attitude on the limited panel.

normally in balance, are one of the best ways of increasing airspeed and going through the red line on the ASI.

Spin recovery

To recover from a spin on instruments:

1. Close the throttle.

2. Look at the turn needle then apply full rudder in the opposite direction to that indicated.

3. Pause slightly, allowing the rudder to take effect, then –

4. Ease the stick forward until the turn needle centres. It may momentarily flick the other way. At that point the spin has stopped.

5. Centralize the rudder without delay.

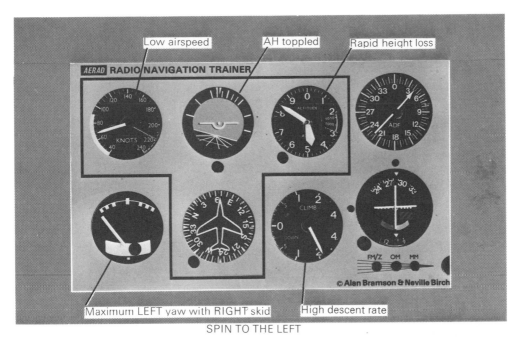

Fig. 19: Comparison of the spin and the spiral dive as seen on instruments.

6. Ease the aircraft gently out of the dive using the procedure already described on pages 70–71.

7. Add cruising or climbing power as required.

Spiral dive recovery

When the instrument panel indicates that the aircraft is in a spiral dive, recover as follows:

1. Close the throttle.

2. Determine the direction of spiral with reference to the turn needle.

3. Apply opposite aileron to the direction indicated on the turn needle.

4. Maintain balance by applying rudder in the direction indicated by the ball.

5. When the turn needle centres take off aileron, ease out of the dive as explained on page 71 and, as the ASI approaches the required speed for cruise or climb, add the appropriate power.

Instrument limitations

While for practical purposes an ASI will give instant readings (it is the time needed for the aircraft to accelerate or decelerate that causes a lag in ASI readings, not the instrument itself), altimeters of the kind fitted to most light aircraft cannot cope with very rapid changes in height. In a fast descent, for example, the altimeter could lag behind aircraft level by 300ft or more. So avoid high-speed let-down in cloud, particularly when the new altitude offers only moderate clearance between you and the highest object below the aircraft.

While Instant Reading VSIs are now fitted as an option to many light singles and twins, not all aircraft have them so do not expect the impossible of these much maligned inhabitants of the flight panel. Intelligently used they can provide valuable back-up information as an aid to maintaining flight level and specific rates of climb or descent.

Most, but not all, modern gyro instruments have complete freedom of movement in each axis but when there are toppling limits do not be surprised if the direction indicator behaves like a roulette wheel after a manoeuvre which takes it beyond limits. The re-set knob should put it instantly back in business but these days Artificial Horizons have no such manual device and it can take ten minutes or more before the pendulous unit re-erects the horizon bar.

Failure of the pressure instruments

If, for any reason, there is a blockage (such as ice) in the pressure head feeding the pressure instruments, and even if there is no alternate static source, you can break the glass of the VSI. It will then give readings in the reverse direction (i.e. UP when you are in fact descending) and the altimeter will provide moderately accurate indications. This break-the-glass procedure only works in non-pressurized aircraft but pressurized equipment is in any case always provided with more than one pressure/static system.

The importance of practice

Earlier in this chapter I stated that basic instrument flying is the building block of radio navigation but of course no instrument is better than the man who uses it. Until the pilot can fly on instruments as if conditions were VMC, he can hardly expect to cope with IMC when there are charts to find, radios to tune and controllers to chat up. The only answer to gaining the necessary skills in basic instrument flying is practice, practice and more practice. There are no short cuts, only a few training aids aimed at reducing the cost, such as simulator flying and playing with 'adjust by hand' instrument panels of the type used for some of the illustrations in this chapter.

Radio commands

While the Basic 'T' instruments enable a competent pilot to fly his aircraft at a prescribed flight level, heading and speed, it is the radio instruments that provide the necessary commands telling him what numbers should appear on his flight panel. As far as pilot technique is concerned radio aids fall into two categories:

a) Pilot interpreted: The pilot flies with reference to the flight instruments in order to conform with commands from the radio instruments (i.e. VOR, ILS, ADF, DME, etc.).

b) Ground monitored: One or more communications transceiver is installed in the aircraft and information is passed to the pilot by a radar or VDF controller. The only additional airborne equipment that will enhance the value of radar is a transponder.

In each class of radio aid the principle is the same. On a pilot-interpreted aid a needle or digital display tells the pilot whether he is on a correct flight path or if he has departed from it. In the case of a ground-monitored system the friendly voice of the controller performs the same function by issuing a statement such as 'you are slightly to the left of centreline, range five miles, height should be one-five-five-zero feet'.

Applying the commands to the instruments

Among inexperienced instrument pilots the most common weaknesses in radio navigation procedures are:

1. Failure to allow for the wind.

2. Inability to picture the situation being indicated by the radio instruments.

3. A tendency to steer headings on the ADF or VOR instead of using the direction indicator.

4. Failure to anticipate the next move, particularly when readings are altering fast.

Here are some useful tricks of the trade which should prove of value.

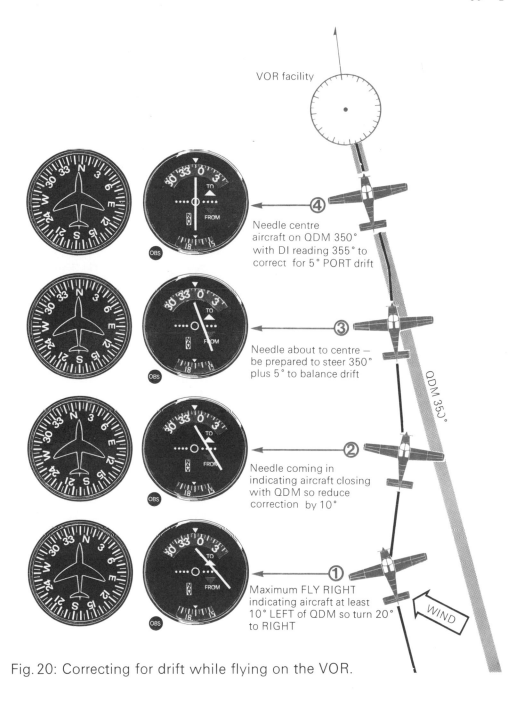

VOR facility

④ Needle centre aircraft on QDM 350° with DI reading 355° to correct for 5° PORT drift

③ Needle about to centre — be prepared to steer 350° plus 5° to balance drift

② Needle coming in indicating aircraft closing with QDM so reduce correction by 10°

① Maximum FLY RIGHT indicating aircraft at least 10° LEFT of QDM so turn 20° to RIGHT

QDM 350°

WIND

Fig. 20: Correcting for drift while flying on the VOR.

Combating wind effect

VOR

When tracking to or from the facility if the needle drifts left or right make a 10 degree correction on the DI and give it time to have effect. Hold the new heading on the DI and adjust the correction as necessary (Fig. 20).

ADF

When tracking to or from the facility remember the needle always points to the NDB. Imagine you are approaching the beacon on a QDM of 270 degrees when after a few moments the radio compass needle moves from 0 degrees to 350 degrees indicating that the NDB is slightly to the left of the nose. Obviously you have drifted to the right and the wind is from the left (Fig. 21). Turn left 25 degrees and hold 245 degrees on the DI. The radio compass will now indicate 015 degrees and unless the wind is very strong the needle will gradually increase its reading as the aircraft regains the QDM. This will be when 025 degrees is indicated by the radio compass because if, at this stage, the aircraft were turned right through 25 degrees the radio compass would read zero and the DI would indicate 270 degrees. Having regained the QDM it only remains to maintain it by turning right until the DI reads 260 degrees and the radio compass is showing 010 degrees. In this example 10 degrees of drift is being corrected and adjustments may have to be made as the flight proceeds, but the important thing to remember is to steer on the DI – *not* the radio compass.

ADF hold in a crosswind (Fig. 22)

This is one of the exercises that sorts the men out from the boys but the rules of the game are relatively simple:

1.   Find the drift angle while flying inbound. Note it down.

2.   Treble the drift and apply it in the reverse direction while flying outbound.

The ILS

It should be remembered that whereas full needle deflection on the VOR

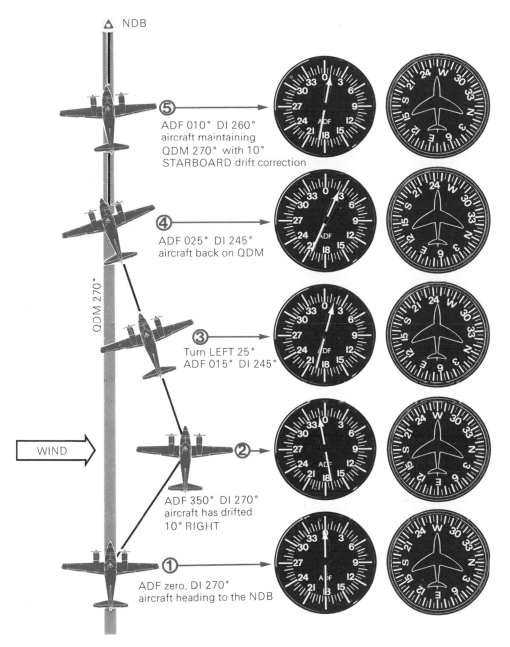

NDB

⑤
ADF 010° DI 260°
aircraft maintaining
QDM 270° with 10°
STARBOARD drift correction

④
ADF 025° DI 245°
aircraft back on QDM

③
Turn LEFT 25°
ADF 015° DI 245°

QDM 270°

WIND

②
ADF 350° DI 270°
aircraft has drifted
10° RIGHT

①
ADF zero, DI 270°
aircraft heading to the NDB

Fig. 21: Correcting for drift while flying to the NDB.

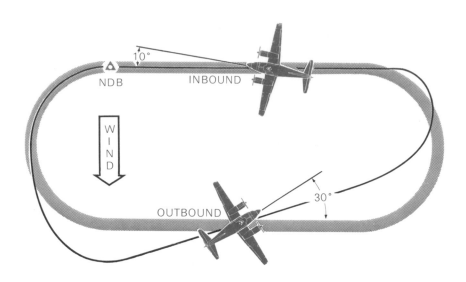

Fig. 22: The ADF hold in a crosswind.

represents about 10 degrees, a similar indication while flying the ILS localizer means you are only 2.5 degrees off runway centreline, and from maximum FLY UP to maximum FLY DOWN represents a trifling 1.2 degrees. Clearly the crosspointers used in conjunction with ILS are very sensitive and do not take kindly to the from-crisis-to-crisis style of flying.

When a needle makes the slightest move go after it. This is no time to wait for the situation to get out of hand. When there is a small departure from glide path use the elevators for minor corrections. A persistent FLY UP or FLY DOWN command will, of course, require a combination of elevator and small power adjustments.

If the aircraft drifts, say, two dots to the left alter heading on the direction indicator by 5 degrees. Remember each dot represents about 0.5 degrees so all heading corrections must be small.

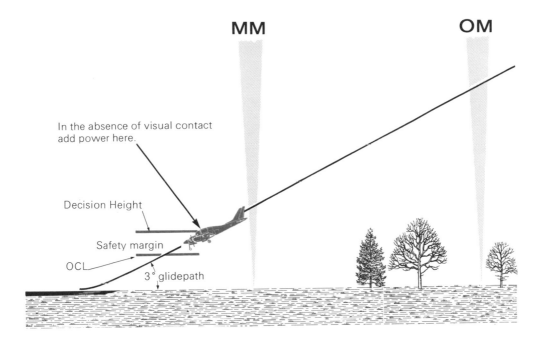

MM   **OM**

In the absence of visual contact
add power here.

Decision Height

Safety margin

OCL

3° glidepath

Fig. 23: Adding power as Decision Height is approached (see below).

Decision Heights

In the absence of company rulings it is common practice to calculate Decision Height by taking the published OCL (Obstacle Clearance Limit) for the aid being used and, in the case of light aircraft, adding a 6oft safety margin. If you are making an instrument approach and have not established visual contact at Decision Height, power must be added and a 'Missed Approach' started immediately (Fig. 23). It is the height of folly to descend below OCL.

Instrument flying makes heavy demands on the pilot and in the early stages of training it can be very exhausting. But as your skill increases with practice much of the sweat evaporates from the various procedures and I/F becomes routine. Nonetheless, the traps are many (wrong altimeter settings, incorrect radio frequencies etc.) and it is a branch of flying that does not suffer fools gladly.

5. CROSSWIND TAKE-OFF AND LANDING

Within living memory landing speeds, and by that I mean speeds at point of touchdown, have increased to double the cruise performance of early passenger aircraft and perhaps to three times the cruising speeds of light 'planes of the mid 1920s. Both this fact and the remarkable growth in weight that has gone hand in hand with progress, made it only a matter of time before the grass airfield had to disappear from the scene as far as passenger and freight operations were concerned.

However, one of the charms of the grass airfield is that it provides a great variety of take-off and landing directions – that is, until those in charge start marking out runways, which confine all traffic to a small proportion of the field and so remove this great advantage. The advent of runways, hard or grass, has brought with it limitation of take-off and landing directions. Modern aircraft, big and small, are better able to cope with the situation than the old designs, but it is nevertheless more important for pilots to know how to deal with crosswinds than it was in the days when they could pick their own direction with reference to the wind sock. Nowadays only a very few of the old-style of grass airfield that did not masquerade as an airport still exist.

The crosswind battle was by no means one-sided. For example, at one time Goodyear marketed their Castoring Undercarriage – a device capable of providing endless entertainment to pilots and onlookers alike. You could taxi like there was a bomb behind you, then put on a bootful of rudder whereupon the aircraft would career more or less sideways, in a direction bearing little resemblance to where the nose was pointing. The idea was that pilots could land or take off in a crosswind without the tedium of having to acquire skill. Now I am not one of those who believes in doing things the hard way but any pilot who needs castoring under-carriages when the wind ceases to oblige by blowing down the runway should, in my view, turn to other things. It is, after all, a fact that at most airfields occasions when the wind is actually blowing down the centre-line can be counted on the fingers of one hand.

The effects of crosswinds

Drift and the landing gear

Most undercarriages are fairly robust affairs, but they are primarily designed to support the weight of the aircraft and to absorb shock in the vertical plane. Similarly, the main landing gear struts are required to withstand the longitudinal retarding force that follows application of the brakes. Sideways loads are another matter and clearly there is a limit to the amount that the landing gear can tolerate. Put into the simplest terms, wheels are not designed to move sideways and even a relatively small drift component amounting to 5–10 knots can have a disastrous effect on the landing gear structure.

Fig. 24 shows the displacement from runway centreline which occurs when no attempt is made during the hold-off to compensate for the effects of a modest 5 knot crosswind. Two problems are apparent:

1. The runway is departed before the actual touchdown.

2. Touchdown occurs with a 5 knot sideways velocity and that would most likely wreck the landing gear.

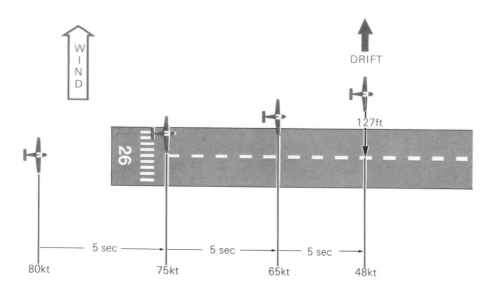

Fig. 24: Drift effect when no attempt is made to compensate for a 5 knot crosswind while landing. Imagine the strain on the landing gear on touchdown.

Crosswind limits

Before revising the correct take-off and landing techniques applicable to crosswind conditions I want to say a word about limits. Not all aircraft have the same degree of tolerance. Some can cope with relatively strong crosswind components while others, under similar conditions, will threaten to turn round and bite their own tails. The strange thing is that aircraft size is not, in itself, the deciding factor. Some light singles have higher crosswind limits than much larger and heavier twins. In calculating the limit on any specific occasion the two factors to take into account are:

1. Wind speed.

2. Wind direction relative to aircraft take-off or landing path.

Wind speed alone does not provide sufficient information for the pilot to decide if it is safe to attempt a take-off or landing. Obviously the wind will have most drift effect when it is at 90 degrees to the take-off or landing path and will produce progressively less drift as it lines up more closely with the fore and aft axis of the aircraft (Fig. 25).

Flight/Operating Manual information on crosswind limits ranges from a simple statement to the effect that the Maximum Demonstrated Crosswind Velocity is *x* knots (at 90 degrees to the aircraft), to a diagram such as that shown in Fig. 26. This makes it a simple matter for the pilot to compute the wind component acting at 90 degrees to the aircraft (shown on the Wind Component Graph as 'Wind Component Perpendicular to Runway'). So if you are sitting on Runway 27 and they advise a surface wind of 310/40 knots you know there is a 40 knot wind blowing at an angle of 40 degrees to the take-off direction. A quick look at the Wind Component Graph will show that the actual wind strength at 90 degrees to the aircraft is 26 knots. And the decision to take off or taxi back to the hanger will depend on whether or not 26 knots crosswind (90 degrees of it) are within limits for the aircraft.

The crosswind take-off (Fig. 27)

Assuming that conditions are within aircraft limits and you decide to take off, your main considerations are to prevent the wing (the one into wind) from rising, to keep straight down the runway and to contain any tendency for the aircraft to drift sideways.

So long as the wheels remain firmly in contact with the runway there is little chance of drift unless there is rain, snow or ice to contend with. There is, however, a danger that the aircraft might lift off momentarily, start drifting, then sink back on to the ground with expensive results, and you must guard against this eventuality at all costs. Here is the procedure to adopt:

1. Line up on the runway and be absolutely clear about the direction of crosswind, left or right.

2. Apply aileron into wind, i.e. when the wind is from the left, move

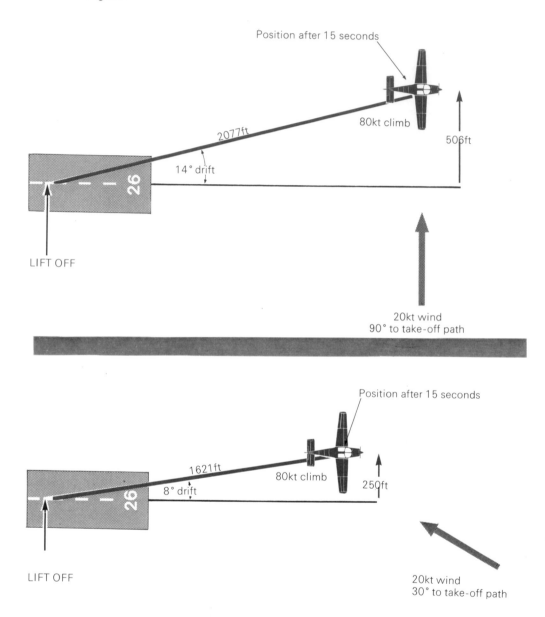

Fig. 25: Effect of wind direction on climb path. The illustrations assume the pilot holds the runway QDM after lift-off.

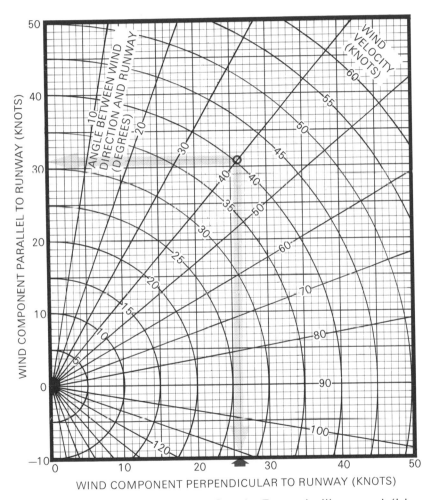

Fig. 26: Typical Wind Component Graph. Example illustrated (blue arrows) shows that when a 40 knot wind is blowing at 40 degrees to the take-off or landing path wind strength at 90 degrees to the aircraft will be 26 knots. Aircraft Manuals will advise if this is within limits.

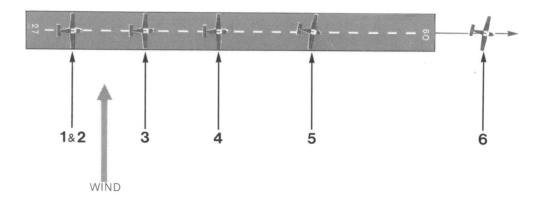

Fig. 27: The crosswind take-off. Numbers against each aircraft relate to the text.

the wheel to the *left* and when the wind is from the right move the wheel to the *right*. In that way the into-wind mainplane will be prevented from lifting as the aircraft accelerates down the runway.

3. When it is clear to take off, open up power and concentrate on keeping straight. Most modern aircraft have adequate nosewheel steering but with certain single-engine designs brake may be required on the side of the aircraft opposite to the wind (e.g. wind from the left, a touch of *right* brake). As speed increases and the rudder becomes more effective there will be no need to supplement it with brake. With some twin-engine aircraft you can help prevent a swing in the early stages of a crosswind take-off by opening up the into-wind engine slightly in advance of the downwind one (e.g. wind from the right, lead with the *right* throttle).

4. Deliberately hold the aircraft on the runway until 5 knots or so

above normal rotate speed, then lift off cleanly. On no account allow the aircraft to sink back on to the ground since drift will start immediately the wheels leave the runway.

5. Maintain runway centreline after lift-off by turning gently into wind so that drift is corrected.

6. Climb away as usual and carry out the normal post-take-off actions.

The crosswind landing

Landing in a crosswind presents the pilot with similar problems to those inherent in the take-off, in that once again he must safeguard the under-carriage by containing drift. However, the crosswind landing generates additional difficulties and these will be dealt with in due course.

Two methods of dealing with out-of-wind landing conditions are accepted practice:

1. The 'crabbing' method.

2. The 'wing-down' method.

Each technique has its champions and I make no attempt to suggest which is the better of the two. In fact some pilots have a habit of combining the 'wing-down' with the 'crab'. Personally I think this makes the exercise unnecessarily complicated and the explanations that follow therefore describe each method separately. But first we must consider the final turn, which is the same for both methods.

The final turn

On the basis that a good approach forms the foundations of a good landing it is vital that the pilot should not have to spend most of his time fighting to line up with the runway while motoring in. In crosswind conditions some pilots reach crisis point and approach the runway at a tangent, usually thumping the hardware down well to one side of the centreline. The

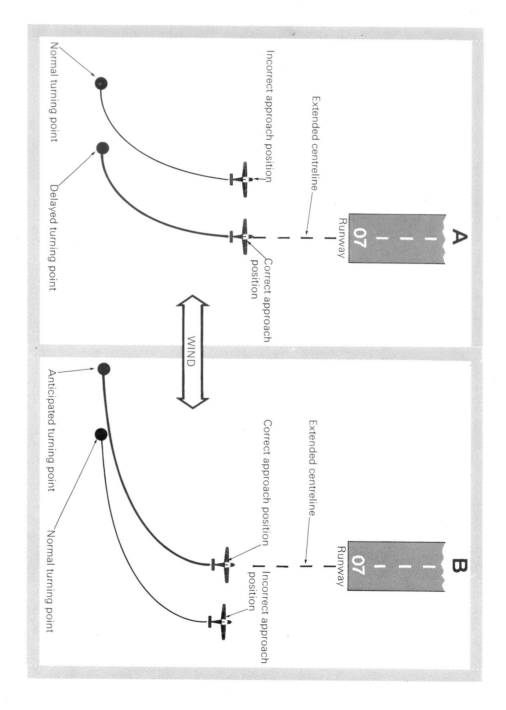

Fig. 28: The final turn in a crosswind. The aircraft approaching Runway A is experiencing port drift and should delay the turn, while the aircraft joining Runway B must start turning early if it is to avoid flying through the extended centreline.

slightest swing away from runway centre and they are on the grass, removing the odd light fitting or marker board for luck.

To avoid this kind of drama, plan ahead. Imagine you are turning on to finals from a left-hand base leg and that on the way in the wind will be from the right. Such a wind will tighten up the radius of turn and could position you to the left of extended centreline (Fig. 28A).

Remedy: Delay the final turn and if necessary widen its radius by reducing the rate of turn (i.e. decrease the bank angle).

On the other hand, picture the same circuit direction but this time with the wind from the left. The result is an increase in turn radius that may well position the aircraft to the right of extended centreline (Fig. 28B).

Remedy: Anticipate the final turn and, if necessary, tighten its radius by increasing the rate of turn (i.e. increase the bank angle).

Having lined up correctly for the approach the next hurdle is the crosswind landing itself, and it is at this stage that you have a choice between the two methods described below.

The crabbing method (Fig. 29)

1. Maintain the descent path along extended runway centreline by turning slightly so that the nose is into the wind. Make corrections by turning away from the drift –

   Aircraft drifting right turn slightly *left*.
   Aircraft drifting left turn slightly *right*.

2. Cross the runway threshold and check there is no drift. The aircraft must be over the centreline. At the usual height initiate the round-out and then take off power.

3. Hold off in the normal way except that the nose will be towards the windward side of the runway. Just before touchdown hold the wings level and apply rudder to *flat-turn* the aircraft along runway centreline.

4. Allow the aircraft to touch down as it aligns with the runway, then apply aileron towards the wind to hold down the wing.

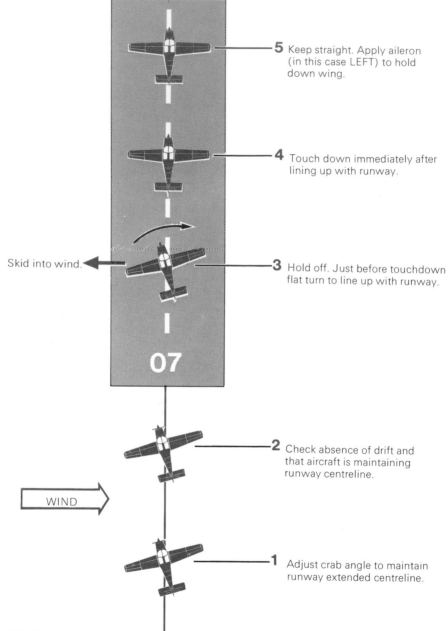

5 Keep straight. Apply aileron
(in this case LEFT) to hold
down wing.

4 Touch down immediately after
lining up with runway.

Skid into wind.

3 Hold off. Just before touchdown
flat turn to line up with runway.

07

2 Check absence of drift and
that aircraft is maintaining
runway centreline.

WIND

1 Adjust crab angle to maintain
runway extended centreline.

Fig. 29: Crosswind landing, crabbing method.

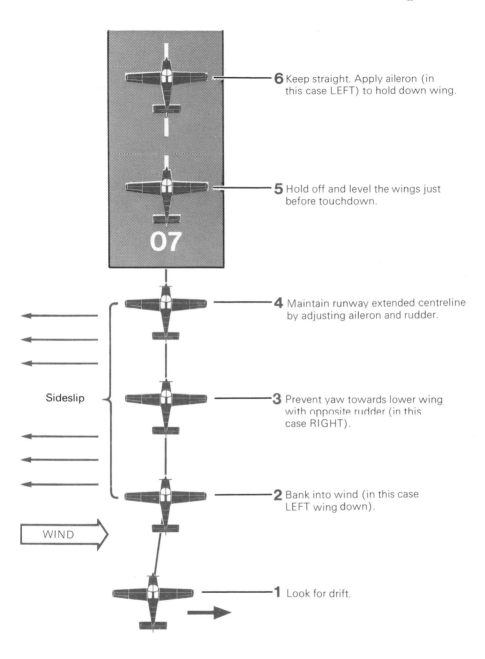

6 Keep straight. Apply aileron (in this case LEFT) to hold down wing.

5 Hold off and level the wings just before touchdown.

4 Maintain runway extended centreline by adjusting aileron and rudder.

Sideslip

3 Prevent yaw towards lower wing with opposite rudder (in this case RIGHT).

2 Bank into wind (in this case LEFT wing down).

WIND

1 Look for drift.

Fig. 30: Crosswind landing, wing-down method.

5. Keep straight during the landing roll using nosewheel steering assisted by brake if necessary. On twin-engine aircraft you may need to use asymmetric throttle under conditions of extreme crosswind.

6. Bring the aircraft to a halt, clear the runway, carry out the post-land checks and then taxi in.

The critical part of this procedure is without doubt the few seconds immediately before touchdown. The pilot faces a dilemma. Either he lands in the direction in which he is pointing, while fighting off drift, and as a result runs off the runway at an angle, or he is at risk of lining up too soon with the runway centreline and allowing drift to develop during the hold-off.

This part of the landing calls for nice timing but, properly executed, the flat turn (made just before touchdown for the purpose of lining up with the runway) will provoke a gentle skid into wind and, for a few seconds at least, will balance drift. An imperfect landing of this kind should at least ensure that you get the minimum of drift on making contact with the ground. Really tidy arrivals, like anything else, require practice.

The wing-down method (Fig. 30)

All the considerations relating to the final turn (page 89) apply to the wing-down procedure and the following step-by-step explanation starts from when the aircraft is on the approach. In this method drift is prevented by using a manoeuvre as old as aviation itself – the sideslip.

1. Turn on to finals making sure that the aircraft is on the runway extended centreline. Look out for drift.

2. When you recognize drift, bank the aircraft in the opposite direction (i.e. into wind).

3. Prevent the aircraft from turning towards the lower wing (due to further effects of aileron) by applying rudder in the opposite direction. The aircraft will now slip into wind.

4. Maintain runway extended centreline by adjusting bank angle, using aileron away from drift. Add rudder if the bank needs to be steeper and take off some rudder when the bank is reduced.

5. Continue down the approach to the round-out, take off power and, just before landing, level the wings.

6. After landing concentrate on keeping straight using nosewheel steering, brake (if required) and, if flying a twin in conditions of strong crosswind, use asymmetric power. Prevent a wing from lifting by applying aileron towards the wind.

7. Clear the runway, carry out the post landing checks then taxi in.

In the days of biplanes it was the practice to land on one wheel and run along the ground, wing down, until the ailerons ran out of steam. Now it is unfashionable to do circus acts of this kind and the aim is to hold the aircraft in a banked attitude until immediately before touchdown. As with the crabbing method, timing is of the essence. Take off the bank too soon and drift will start before the wheels are on the ground. Leave it too late and you will land on one wheel. (Most of us often do in any case. A friend of mine has a habit of shouting 'my side is down' whenever I arrive on one wheel slightly before the other.) Once again practice is the only key to tidy arrivals.

Special warnings

Use of flap

Most aircraft handle better in a crosswind when flap is limited. In a crosswind take-off most flight manuals for those aircraft that normally use 10–15 degrees of flap usually recommend the minimum of flap or no flap at all. In the absence of specific flight manual advice a maximum of half flap will suffice for most aircraft when landing in out-of-wind conditions.

Wheelbarrowing

A word of warning about holding the aircraft on the runway until you reach a higher than usual lift-off speed. At all costs avoid using too much forward pressure on the control yoke because some aircraft, particularly those with all-flying tailplanes (known as stabilators in the USA), are ready and willing to lift off the mainwheels leaving the ironmongery free to run along the ground on its nosewheel. The combined effects of slipstream over the inner portion of the wings, torque and, in particular, the very crosswind we are trying to combat, will almost certainly cause your favourite 'plane to pivot around the nosewheel like an unstable wheelbarrow – hence the term 'wheelbarrowing'. It all happens rather quickly and the experience is guaranteed to entertain anybody watching on the ground from a safe distance.

There are recorded cases of wheelbarrowing having afflicted four-engine passenger aircraft, proving that the phenomenon is not confined to the little ones. If it should happen to you (and it can occur during the landing as well as the take-off) you should aim to plant the mainwheels on the ground without delay. You do that by easing gently back on the elevator control, so removing the weight from nosewheel to mainwheels.

All take-offs and landings demand skill and judgement – particularly when the wind will not cooperate by blowing down the runway. But you should not take the fact that a crosswind take-off or landing demands a little more skill as an excuse for swiping off the landing gear, putting a wing tip into the ground or making other mistakes. Be warned by the accident statistics and think of the insurance and the damage to your standing as a pilot which will result if you make a mess of it. On the other hand your reputation as a pilot will certainly be duly enhanced if you pull off a perfect landing in spite of difficult crosswind conditions.

6. ACHIEVING SAFETY FROM TWO ENGINES

Let me tell you a true story. Once upon a time all aircraft were little ones. They had to be; engines at that time were massive and heavy with hardly enough power to pull the skin off a rice pudding. Then along came the First World War and the demands for bigger and better bomb loads caused airplanes to grow and outstrip engines. To overcome the problem the wise men of aviation decided to fit several engines, and some ponderous aeronautical hardware emerged as a result. There was no question of twin-engine safety in those days. Indeed the complexity of fitting two motors was accepted at the time as the only way to increase power. With both engines running some of the early twins had a climb rate of only 250ft per minute and on one engine they flew like a winged brick.

Over the years the search for more power inspired aircraft with two, three, four and more engines. The fashion reached its high point in 1929 when Dornier, the German aircraft firm, built the DO-X and went into the wholesale engine business. They fitted no fewer than twelve Curtiss Conqueror engines above the wing in six pairs. Fully loaded it was incapable of climbing out of ground effect and rumour has it that during a flight from Cape Verde Islands to Brazil the DO-X flew so near the waves that its passengers were at a loss to decide whether to be seasick or airsick.

It was not until the mid-1930s that aircraft with a reasonable degree of engine-out safety became available. Then came the Second World War and the development of multi-engine bombers and fighters that, in original form, went like a rocket with an engine stopped. I say in original form because it was not long before the demand for more range (i.e. increased fuel) and bigger bomb loads so pushed up the weight of these excellent aircraft that we were back to the 'winged brick' situation of the First World War. A Dakota was manageable on one engine at its designed 25,200lb (11,500kg). At 31,000lb (14,000kg) it was a non-starter. The de Havilland Mosquito would do climbing rolls on one engine, that is until they gave it the same bomb load as a B17 Flying Fortress. Then the take-off and initial climb had to be seen to be believed. They were brave men those Mossie pilots who carried a 4000lb (1800kg) bomb.

Peace arrived and most aviating nations of the world agreed that civil aircraft carrying fare-paying customers would have to be capable of climbing, fully loaded, when an engine quit on take-off. If it could do that the engine-out cruise would, of course, present no problems other than a reduction in operating altitude. However, most readers of this book will not fly large public transport equipment and will be more concerned with light twins, piston-engine and turboprop. Turboprops must usually conform with more stringent certification requirements, but unless they are being used for public transport purposes, light piston-engine twins are not required to climb on one fan at maximum weight.

Many pilots, myself included, regard the certification requirements for light twins as bordering on the inadequate but, fortunately, most of the manufacturers are more responsible than the aviation authorities of the world; you will not find a modern light twin that is incapable of climbing with an engine feathered. However, with the regulations as they are one can hardly expect the leading general aviation firms, operating as they do in a highly competitive world, to give us a sparkling engine-out rate of climb at the expense of payload or range.

The majority of piston-engine twins of less than 12,500lb (5700kg) maximum weight offer a single-engine climb rate of 200–300ft per minute. When the airfield is high, the temperature is fit for sun bathing and there is turbulence a pilot of limited experience or ability would most likely find that his miserable book figure of 200ft or more per minute would translate into a descent, following engine failure after take-off. Airfield elevation depends upon where you fly and you cannot influence the weather, but the other important factor, and the one where this chapter can be of assistance, is pilot skill.

Principles related to asymmetrics

A cynical old fighter pilot who was being converted on to twins once complained that he could see no advantage in having two engines as there was twice as much to go wrong. Nevertheless, properly handled, even those light twins with a marginal single-engine climb rate can provide a high degree of safety and security while flying over mountains, water or any other areas where engine failure would spell disaster to singles. It must, however, be admitted that an engine failure on a twin does all too often result in an accident, but this is not usually the fault of the hardware; it is entirely due to the ignorance of the driver.

Before describing the various procedures let me revise the aerodynamics of engine failure on multis and asymmetric flight. Under normal conditions the situation is as shown in Fig. 31. Thrust is provided in equal halves to provide Total Thrust which is opposed by Total Drag, the two forces acting through aircraft centreline.

Imagine the right-hand engine fails. Immediately Total Thrust moves away from aircraft centreline since it is confined to the port engine. Furthermore, the right-hand engine has ceased to be a donkey and become a passenger – a particularly obstructive one too, until the propeller is feathered. The result? Well, with Total Thrust moving to the left and Total Drag shunting to the right the opposing forces (imagine them as lengths of string pulling on a model aircraft) cause a yaw towards the failed engine (Fig. 32). The events that follow when the aircraft is left to its own devices are these. The yaw produces a roll in the same direction (like 'further effects of rudder') and, since the fuselage is firmly glued to the mainplanes, the nose follows the down-going right wing tip into a spiral dive. It is exactly as though one had put on a bootful of right rudder and left the bird to sort itself without help from the other controls.

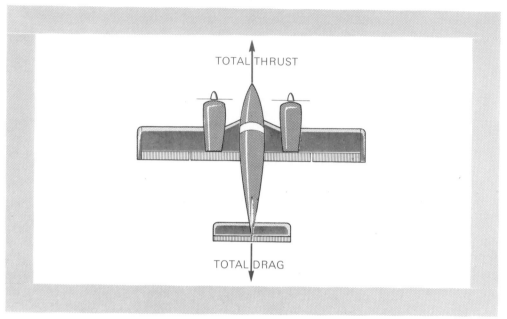

Fig. 31: Total Thrust and Drag in normal flight.

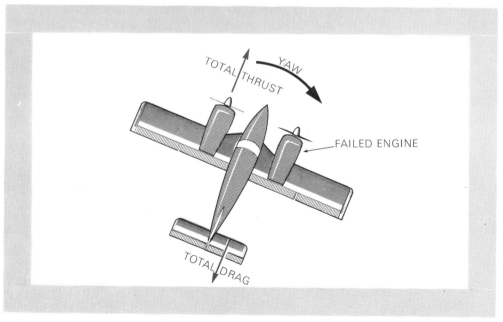

Fig. 32: Total Thrust and Drag, right engine failed.

Minimum control speed

As everyone who has ever received formal twin-conversion training knows, engine failure is dealt with by applying rudder to oppose yaw and so prevent the yaw/roll/spiral dive sequence already described. However, the rudder, like any other flying control, is only as effective as the airflow over it and herein lies the problem. If you let the speed drop too low the rudder will lose its muscle and even the fully outstretched leg will be incapable of combating the yawing force of the live engine, aided and abetted by drag from the one that has failed.

There was a time when we used to talk about 'critical speed' and 'safety speed' in the most general terms. Unfortunately the minimum speed at which it is possible to maintain direction on one engine, known as 'minimum control speed', cannot be quoted as a single figure for any particular aircraft because it varies according to circumstances. Here are the factors that affect it:

1. **Altitude:** Since more power means more asymmetric thrust (and therefore yawing action) it follows that minimum control speed will be at its highest at full throttle altitude where maximum power can be developed.

2. **Load:** A fully loaded aircraft must, speed for speed, fly at a bigger angle of attack than a near empty one of the same type. A bigger angle of attack means more drag, and that in turn demands increased power. So we are back at square one; more power, more yaw and in consequence a higher minimum control speed.

3. **Drag:** This takes us back to point 2. More drag means more power means more yaw, etc. I mention it as a separate item to draw attention to the fact that flying with the cooling flaps open and the landing gear extended will demand more power from the live engine – and will therefore mean an increase in minimum control speed.

4. **Flaps:** This is a complicated one because some flaps give very

little drag increase until after the first 10–15 degrees of depression. As a guideline it is probably best to regard the flaps as coming under the heading of 'Drag' and leave them up, unless the aircraft manual specifically advises otherwise. Obviously flaps will be used during an asymmetric landing, but more about that later.

5. **Windmilling:** While some of the early light twins had fixed pitch propellers these days constant speed/feathering ones are universal. However, the drag from a windmilling propeller is very considerable and since it will provide a great deal of 'anti-thrust' (i.e. drag), minimum control speed will be appreciably higher than usual until it is feathered. Remember that windmilling drag is *asymmetric* drag – and that is Poison (with a capital P).

6. **Pilot limitations:** These days aircraft are blessed with adequate trim, so the pilot should not be hampered by the physical limitation of being unable to apply sufficient rudder. His own skill is another matter and the airframe driver who knows how to fly on one engine will usually achieve a lower minimum control speed than an aviator who does not know what he is about – but that is hardly surprising.

7. **Critical engine:** When both propellers go around in the same direction, slipstream and torque effects have a natural tendency to create yaw. In the case of a modern piston-engine, where the propellers turn clockwise when seen from the rear, the yaw is to the left.

   Naturally, failure of an engine means loss of power and that in turn induces a drop in speed. To maintain height the angle of attack must be increased so that the bird is flying along in a tail-down/nose-up attitude.

   In the tail-down attitude the prop-shafts are inclined upwards and the tops of the propeller discs are therefore tilted backwards. If you think about it, that means the down-going propeller blade (i.e. the one on the right of the disc when seen from behind during

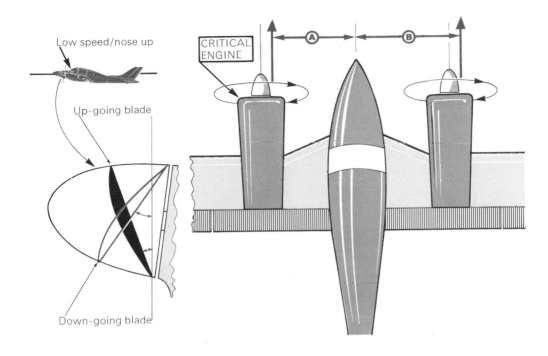

Fig. 33: Critical engine. The smaller drawings on the left show how an inclined propeller disc causes the down-going blade to have a larger pitch angle than the up-going blade (shown in solid black). Because of this, in slow, nose-up flight centres of thrust move to the right. Moment arm A is then shorter than B, therefore failure of the left-hand engine would leave asymmetric power on the side with more leverage, and would be more critical than loss of the right-hand engine.

clockwise rotation) will have a bigger angle than the up-going blade on the other side. Such a situation is known in the trade as Asymmetric Blade Effect. It is a curse well known to pilots taking off in tailwheel aircraft, where, until the tail is raised there is the same problem of the tilted propeller shaft.

Take a look at Fig. 33 and remember we are maintaining height on reduced power in a tail-down flight attitude. Because the down-going blade has an increased angle, more thrust is being generated by the right half of the propeller disc than by the left. In effect the centre of thrust for the left engine has moved towards aircraft centreline while that for the right-hand motor has moved away. The amount of yawing force that can be generated by an engine depends on the amount of thrust and the leverage (or, to be more correct, moment arm), through which it acts. Since moment arm B is longer than moment arm A the right-hand engine will clearly exert more yawing force during engine-out flight than could the left-hand one. Consequently the greater yaw (and therefore the higher minimum control speed) in this instance would result from the loss of the port motor. In other words, when the fans go round clockwise the critical engine is on the left.

It is not always easy to demonstrate a meaningful difference in minimum control speed between the left and right engines, but much ado has been made of the subject. In any case some popular light twins now have counter-rotating propellers, the left one turning clockwise and the right one anti-clockwise, when minimum control speed is the same for both engines.

The 'V' code

The matter of minimum control speed has been further complicated by the introduction of jet aircraft. Compared with piston-engines, even the relatively economical fan jet drinks fuel as though there were a hole in the tank. Consequently a very considerable proportion, perhaps more than 53 per cent, of the total weight of a large passenger jet may be fuel. For example, the Super VC 10 may start a long journey weighing 350,000lb (152,000kg) and arrive at the destination with a gross of only 159,000lb (72,000kg). From the pilot's point of view these are two different aircraft and obviously such radical variations in weight will have a profound effect on minimum control as well as on all other speeds. For instance, Target Threshold Speed for this aircraft at maximum landing weight is 166 knots. At the end of the trip it could be 113 knots – light twin speed! To cater for these variables, some of which have already been mentioned, a schedule of speeds has been evolved with definitions that are (more or less) internationally agreed. This, of course, is our old friend the 'V' code.

Many of the speeds listed in this now quite lengthy code are primarily of interest to aircraft designers and test pilots, and are of little concern to most of us involved in light and general aviation. The more important ones that are likely to interest readers of this book are as follows:

V_1 **Decision speed during take-off:** Up to that speed there should be enough runway for the aircraft to stop if, for any reason, you decide to abandon the take-off. Beyond V_1 you are committed to press on and blast off on one engine.

V_r **Rotate speed:** At this stage the nose should be lifted to attain the take-off attitude.

V_2 **Take-off safety speed:** This is, in fact, minimum control speed with an added safety margin to cater for the following factors which could apply when an engine fails during or immediately after take-off:

    a) Element of surprise;
    b) Failure of the critical engine;
    c) Landing gear down, flaps in take-off position, propeller windmilling;
    d) Pilot of average strength and ability.

Provided the aircraft has attained V_2 it should be possible to maintain direction and height while things are sorted out.

V_{mcg} **Minimum control speed, ground:** Should an engine fail during take-off but while the 'plane is still on the ground, this is the minimum speed at which direction can be maintained. Some aircraft with good nosewheel steering can handle the situation at any speed provided the nosewheel is in contact with the ground.

V_{mca} **Minimum control speed, air:** This is the minimum speed at which it is possible to maintain direction after failure of the critical engine. No safety allowance is made for any of the items in V_2 so it is of little practical value other than for demonstration purposes while training multi-engine pilots.

V_{mcl} **Minimum control speed, landing:** This is the lowest speed at which it is possible to maintain direction when full power is applied following failure of the critical engine while in the landing configuration. This speed is important since it relates to the asymmetric overshoot (see page 115).

V_{ne} **Never exceed speed:** The ASI should be marked with a red radial line at this speed.

V_{no} **Normal operating speed:** Sometimes called 'maximum structural cruising speed' this is the top of the green arc marked on the ASI. Beyond that speed we enter the yellow or cautionary area which must be avoided while flying in turbulence.

V_y **Speed for best rate of climb.**

V_{yse} **Speed for best engine-out rate of climb:** This should be marked on the ASI as a blue radial line, and is often known as the 'blue line' speed.

V_{fe} **Maximum flap extension speed.**

V_{le} **Maximum landing gear extension speed.**

Overloading

Many of the accidents that afflict multi-engine pilots are the result of over-loading. The short answer to this problem is *don't do it*. Because, if you push your luck in that direction, the miserable engine-out rate of climb offered by most light twins will disappear without trace.

Zero thrust

There was a time when we used to shut down engines during training and practise real engine-out landing. Sad to relate there were equally real accidents, so these days feathering an engine below a minimum height while training is discouraged by most aviation authorities. The minimum feathering height for most light twins is 3000ft agl. Below that height zero thrust should be used on the 'dead' engine and the aircraft manual will often give the manifold pressure for that setting. Usually the figure quoted is around 11–12in but it is easy to find the zero thrust setting by using this method.

1. Above minimum height for an engine shut-down, stop an engine and feather the propeller.

2. Trim the rudder so that balance is maintained (ball) with the feet off the pedals.

3. With the rudder trim in that position re-start the 'failed' engine.

4. Adjust the throttle on the 'failed' engine (i.e. the one you have just re-started) until balance is shown on the slip indicator (ball). Your feet must be off the rudder pedals.

5. Note the manifold pressure on the 'dead' engine for future use. This is the zero thrust setting.

Coping with engine failure

There is no such thing as a good time to have an engine failure but obviously certain phases of flight are more critical than others. For example, when an engine gives up the struggle at a safe cruising altitude there is usually all the time in the world to try and get it re-started. A motor that gives a heart-rending gurgle followed by a decisive bang just after lift-off is another matter, and one that requires your earnest attention, even if it means interrupting a fascinating conversation with the person on your right.

It is, of course, very much better to prevent such dramas altogether and here we are back to pre-flight and engine checks (pages 32 to 38). A growing trap, which is likely to get worse as more and more aircraft fly on turbine engines and Avgas becomes hard to obtain in certain parts of the world, is incorrect re-fuelling. There have been too many cases of turbine fuel (Avtur) being poured into piston-engine aircraft, and on each occasion the bird has registered its protest by going horribly quiet immediately after take-off. True enough, whoever poured in the wrong fuel was a careless idiot, but it is nonetheless the pilot's responsibility to ensure that the appropriate type and amount of fuel has been loaded into the correct tanks. On some aircraft the tip tanks are the auxiliaries – on others they are the 'mains'. So let us be in no doubt. Tell the re-fueller what you want, how much you require and in which tank it is to go. If you are unable to wait and see for yourself what he is doing carefully check the tanks on your return to the aircraft.

Before lift-off

You have carried out all the pre-take-off vital actions and power checks and the take-off roll is under way when, at a speed below V_{mca}, an engine stops. The correct procedure is as follows.

1. Maintain direction, if necessary using brake to assist nosewheel steering.

2. Close both throttles.

3. Move both mixture controls to idle cut-off. Turn off the ignition and fuel.

4. If there is risk of departing the end of the runway, deliberately steer on to the grass – avoiding such obstacles as lights, approach indicators etc.

After lift-off

For large aircraft V_1, V_r and V_2 are found on a series of performance graphs which take into account runway length, airfield elevation, surface and gradient, temperature, wind and aircraft weight. Aircraft of 12,500lb (57,000kg) weight or less are not required to conform with this procedure but the Flight/Owners/Operating Manual will recommend a lift-off speed. This will be at least V_{mca} and it is usually followed by an initial climbing speed. In effect this is another way of ensuring that the aircraft will be

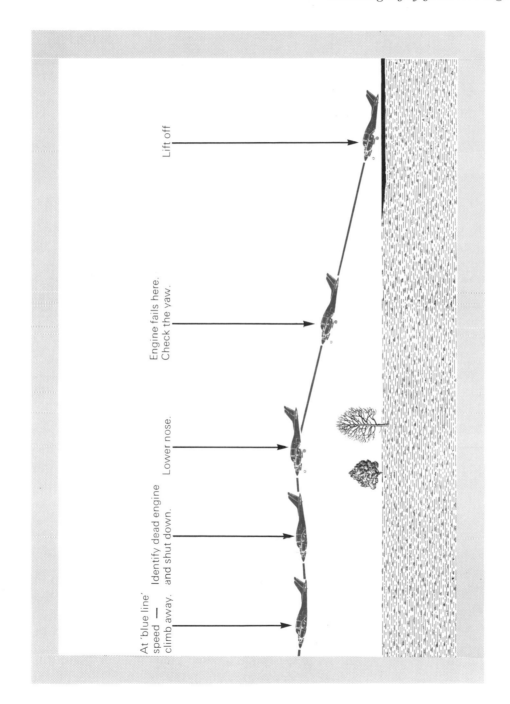

At 'blue line'
speed —
climb away.

Identify dead engine
and shut down.

Lower nose.

Engine fails here.
Check the yaw.

Lift off

Fig. 34: Engine failure after take-off in a twin-engine aircraft.

controllable in the event of engine failure at an embarrassing moment.

So you have accelerated to at least V_{mca} (with perhaps another 5 knots for the wife and kids), the aircraft has lifted off, you have hit 'blue line' speed (best engine-out rate of climb speed) when an engine dies a death (Fig. 34).

1. Immediately check the yaw with rudder and if necessary assist with a little aileron in the same direction.

2. Simultaneously lower the nose to the level flight attitude. It is a common fault to sit there with a windmilling engine, nose pointing to outer space while the ASI winds down like a broken clock. Even if there is a small loss of height it is vital that you maintain speed and keep the rudder in business.

3. Identify the failed engine. Say out aloud 'Dead leg – Dead engine' (i.e. the failed motor is adjacent to the leg that is not pushing). Deliberately touch the throttle of the dead engine, confirm that it is on the same side as the 'dead leg' then move it back. The other engine should keep running and confirm you have pulled the correct lever. Next feather the engine. By doing things in that order you will guard against shutting down the live engine and precipitating the loudest silence known to any pilot! Finally, pull back the mixture control to ICO.

4. At 'blue line' speed climb away, trim as necessary and advise ATC that you have a problem and will be coming back for a landing.

While flying around the circuit watch the temperatures and pressures on the live engine. Treat it kindly; you only have one donkey now and it has to get you back on the runway so use the cowl flaps (if fitted) to avoid overheating. And let up on the power at the first opportunity.

During the cruise

In the bad old days, when few twins would fly satisfactorily on one engine, there was no messing about when half the power went on strike. The shortest measurable length of time was that between failure of the engine and feathering its propeller, even when it happened at a safe height.

These days even light twins of relatively low power will, under normal circumstances, maintain height on one fan although naturally their single-engine ceiling will be lower than that applicable to flight on two engines. Consequently when an engine fails on a modern twin while in the cruise there is plenty of time to think and investigate. It may well be possible to re-start the offending motor. The emergency should be dealt with under two headings: first the *immediate actions*, carried out for the purpose of maintaining control and investigating the situation, and then the *subsequent actions*, which are aimed at setting up the aircraft to fly safely towards an early landing.

Like engine failure during take-off, engine failure in the cruise is one of those situations where checklists have little value in the early stages. You are too occupied getting things under control to be turning the pages and having a read. By all means use a list as a double check after you have dealt with the problem, but your first response to a sudden power loss will have to be done as a drill. Drills must be practised and remembered and one of the best aide-memoires when you are up against it is the mnemonic. Here is one you will find works very nicely for an engine failure while en route. The purists might complain that I have bent the rules of mnemonics slightly by not arranging for each letter to represent an aircraft part or system but who is perfect these days?

a) Immediate Action (Mnemonic: PAID OFF)

P.   Prevent yaw with rudder and if necessary assist with aileron.

A.   Attain engine-out cruising speed.

I.   Identify the failed engine. (Say out loud 'Dead leg – Dead engine'. Remember the 'loud silence' that will result from shutting down the live one!)

D.   Decide whether or not to feather. If there are expensive noises coming from the engine, clouds of smoke, or gushings of oil, or if a conrod has poked its way out of the engine nacelle, take the hint – that motor is not going to start and you must shut it down immediately. On the other hand when the propeller is windmilling noiselessly around it may be possible to re-start the engine. Before investigating –

O.   Open up power on the live engine. We do not want to lose height.

F.   Find the cause of engine failure. Check:
      Ignition ON
      Carb. heat HOT
      Mixture RICH
      Fuel Pressure NORMAL, if not –
      Electric Pump ON (the mechanical fuel pump could have failed).
      Close the throttle and slowly re-open in an effort to restore power. If the engine will not start –

F.   Feather. Deliberately touch the throttle to the dead engine. Slowly close it (checking that the live engine continues running), then feather the propeller, move the mixture to ICO and turn off the ignition.

The immediate action need take no more than thirty seconds. Now for the second half of the procedure.

b) Subsequent actions (Mnemonic: STAR)

S.   Safeguard vacuum and electrics. Turn off all unnecessary electric load when the only remaining alternator/generator is unable to keep its head above water.

T.   Tanks as required. Leave them alone if there is a nearby airfield. Crossfeed when required. (Make sure you know how to crossfeed as now is not the time to find out.)

A.   Airframe clean-up. Close all windows and cowl flaps (if fitted), and check the flaps are fully up. There must be no unnecessary drag. If your 'plane has air conditioning, this is a luxury you will have to forego, as when it is in use, part of it hangs in the breeze, and our one and only engine has enough to do without contending with that. During the airframe clean-up check the trim. An out-of-trim aircraft means constant control corrections; and that can add a lot of drag.

R.   Revise the flight plan and advise ATC of your circumstances.

Now that we have got ourselves organized for safe flight on one engine it only remains to join the circuit and land at the nearest suitable airfield.

The asymmetric landing

While flying towards the airfield make frequent checks on the live engine's temperatures and pressures. On no account push it to the point where things look as though they might go on the boil. Advise the destination that you are on one engine so that other pilots can be warned that they may have to clear the circuit and let you in.

Now plan your joining and circuit procedures because this is no time for the aircraft to get ahead of the pilot. Complete all the checks well in advance and plan a circuit that is large enough to allow time for thought, action and manoeuvre. In their urgency to get in, many pilots crowd themselves, fly through runway extended centreline on the final turn and never get really settled on the approach. If anything, it is better to have a slightly larger circuit than usual. The correct procedure is as follows (see Fig. 35).

1.   Plan the circuit and join at a convenient place (in this example, downwind).

2.   Complete the pre-landing checks but, when the type is known to have a marginal engine-out performance with the wheels lowered, delay these until just before the turn on to base leg. Avoid doing part checks ('Landing gear – I'll lower that later') because later you may forget. Complete the checks all together.

3.   Check temperatures and pressures on the live engine. If things look as though it too is going to quit warn the tower that you are about to

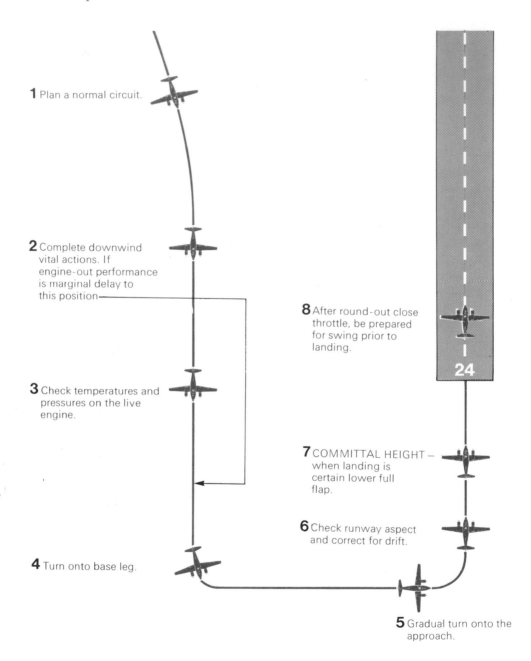

1 Plan a normal circuit.

2 Complete downwind vital actions. If engine-out performance is marginal delay to this position

3 Check temperatures and pressures on the live engine.

8 After round-out close throttle, be prepared for swing prior to landing.

7 COMMITTAL HEIGHT – when landing is certain lower full flap.

6 Check runway aspect and correct for drift.

4 Turn onto base leg.

5 Gradual turn onto the approach.

Fig. 35: The asymmetric circuit and landing.

become a glider and prepare for a curtailed, curved approach. Because of the variables involved, no hard and fast advice can be given in a text book of this kind but clearly this is one of those situations that sorts the men out from the boys.

4.   Turn on to base leg then lower part flap

5.   Start a *gradual* turn on to finals.

6.   Correct for drift and adjust the glide path on the live engine. Aim to approach slightly higher than usual so that not too much power is required. Check the speed and if necessary re-trim.

7.   At Committal Height (500ft for most light twins but check the aircraft manual) decide if it is a 'go' situation. If so, lower full flap (crosswind conditions excepted).

8.   After the round-out be prepared for the aircraft to swing towards the live engine as power is reduced (assuming that rudder loads have been trimmed out on the approach).

Having pulled off a classic asymmetric landing be sure the aircraft is capable of taxiing on one engine before you get yourself into a corner. It would be a pity to bend the 'plane at this stage.

The asymmetric overshoot

While an engine-out overshoot is not the end of the world clearly it should be avoided if at all possible. Imagine the situation. You are on the way in, a feathered propeller on one side, a live engine on the other. Part flap has been applied and the landing gear is locked down. If for any reason it is not possible to land, full power will have to be applied on the live engine, flaps and wheels must come up and the transition from descent to climb will follow. All this takes time and, in the situation described, time means height loss – hence the fixing of a Committal Height below which you must press on and land.

The dangers of approaching at a speed below V_{mcl} are clear. Apply full power and it will not be possible to control the yaw that follows. In most aircraft V_{mcl} plus a small safety margin approximates to 'blue line' speed and during an asymmetric approach, *below that figure thou shall not go*.

Reasons for having to overshoot on one engine can be pilot-induced (coming in too high, too fast for the runway, or not in line with the centre-line etc.) or some ace may have taxied on to the runway believing he could clear out of the way in time. Whatever the reason, when an over-shoot cannot be avoided here is the procedure:

1. Check you are not below the recommended Committal Height.

2. Check the ASI. If you are below 'blue line' speed lower the nose slightly, even if this entails some loss of height.

3. Open up full power on the live engine.

4. Check the yaw with rudder and assist with aileron if necessary.

5. Raise the landing gear.

6. Raise the flaps. In aircraft with unpleasant trim changes it may be prudent to do this in stages, re-trimming at intervals.

7. Start a gentle climb but on no account allow the speed to decrease below 'blue line'.

8. Continue climbing straight ahead but watch the temperatures and pressures on the live engine. It may be flat-rated for continuous full throttle operation but so was the other one now playing passenger with its prop at rest.

9. At a safe height, level out and fly around the circuit for another landing.

Order of clean-up

Opinions differ as to which clean-up action has priority when an engine fails after lift-off, or during the approach. Think of the drag caused by that windmilling propeller. Furthermore it is asymmetric drag trying to yaw the aircraft into a spiral dive, so feather it as a matter of urgency. The wheels and, if used, flaps can be cleaned up later.

Having said all this one should remember that the modern light twin is inherently safe, and it is usually only incompetent pilots that are the danger.

7. AVOIDING WEATHER-INDUCED ACCIDENTS

The 'weather-induced accident' to give it its official name, has now become the commonest cause of fatal incidents in aviation. The odd thing is that the increase in weather accidents has not been confined to particular countries with bad weather or without suitable radio aids. The phenomenon afflicted Britain at the same time as it did South Africa, France, Australia and, of course, the USA.

On the face of it, fewer pilots should these days be getting themselves killed in bad weather, as even the smallest light 'planes are now equipped with radio, some of them to full airways standard. Of course the world pilot population has increased greatly, but the alarming thing is that the proportion of fatal weather-induced accidents has risen in many countries. So here we have an apparent contradiction. On the one hand small aircraft are better equipped and more reliable than ever before, while on the other side of the balance sheet there is evidence of more fatalities per flying hour than in the days when radio was something for the airline pilots – a luxury beyond the reach of single-engine drivers and not all that comprehensive in many of the light twins.

Part of the trouble may lie in the excellence of modern avionics. Over the period when weather accidents grew to their present alarming proportions many pilots became complacent about low cloud, reduced visibility and even icing risks. For were not the little 'black boxes' there to protect them? Certainly the equipment is effective, reasonably reliable and easy to use. But the truth of the matter is we are back to that hard fact of life again. The aircraft may be knee-deep in radio aids and ice protection, but unless the gentleman in the left-hand seat has the necessary skill to use them he might as well switch off and go by train.

People expect too much of aircraft. Sea and road transport may grind to a halt in fog and storms can drive big ships into harbour. But aircraft, big and small, are expected to fly on come hell and high water. In many respects a 'plane is more vulnerable than other means of transport to adverse weather. It is fast, it cannot stop and its multi-dimensional freedom of movement, an asset under normal circumstances, becomes something of a liability when outside visual references fail to appear until the pilot is very near the surface. At this stage he may not like what he sees – and by then it could be too late to do anything about it!

The various human problems listed on page 16 have a bearing on these weather-induced accidents but often the root cause is over-confidence or lack of awareness born of insufficient knowledge. They carried out a survey in the UK and found that over a ten year period more than 33 per cent of all fatal accidents were weather-induced, and the percentage is rising. Only one of these accidents occurred during take-off and not many while landing. The great majority (in fact 67 per cent) occurred while flying en route. In more than half of the cases mentioned the aircraft had flown into ground that was higher than the general terrain. The various accident reports claimed that weather conditions at the time precluded safe operations under VFR. Since only one pilot killed himself during the take-off phase it would seem that most aviators do not deliberately blast off into weather of a hostile nature. Indeed the clear indication is that the pilots involved were overtaken by events, and then elected to press on into worsening conditions although common sense demanded a diversion or a return to base. A more detailed study of the UK reports, which I suspect are typical of most countries, reveals the following contributing factors:

1.   Failure to obtain route and landing forecasts.

2.   Lack of pre-flight preparation.

3. Inability to form a mental picture of the expected flying conditions from a weather report or forecast.

4. Little understanding of the term Minimum Safe Altitude.

5. Refusal to turn back when the pilot has no instrument qualifications, and it is unsafe to rely on visual contact alone.

7. Attempts to climb through cloud by pilots without an instrument qualification.

7. Little understanding of the facilities available to assist pilots in avoiding bad weather.

8. 'Get-home-I-must' frame of mind which overrules caution in the face of obvious danger.

9. Insufficient knowledge of icing and the risk it presents to airframe, engine, radio and instruments.

10. Misuse of the radio equipment.

11. Ignoring the possible effect of down draughts while flying near large, man-made structures or in mountainous regions.

12. Not allowing sufficient clearance from thunderstorms.

Some of these factors have already been mentioned in previous chapters while others are self-evident, but a few of them are worth amplifying.

Translating a weather report into a visual picture

Some very good books have been written on meteorology so there is no point in going over the basics here. What will concern us, however, is how pilots use the equipment, aids and services that are provided for their own safety. So first a word or two about weather report appreciation. Most states have a meteorological service and the information provided is, with minor variations, universal in presentation. You should get the same type

Over the top — a pilot's view of cloud formation that can provide valuable
advance information on likely weather changes.

of charts and print-outs in Germany, France and Belgium as they give at Detroit Metro or London Gatwick. At this stage the questions you should be asking are:

1. Can I read and understand a synoptic chart?

2. Teleprinters push out line after line of letters and figures that are really only fit for use by other teleprinters. Do I understand how to interpret this vital weather information?

3. Do I know the difference between TAFS (Terminal Area Forecasts), Area Forecasts, Route Forecasts, Sigmets and Airmets?

4. Do I appreciate the significance of temperature and its relationship to the Dew Point?

5. Do I understand the meaning of Freezing Level and Icing Index?

6. Do I know how to obtain weather information?

7. When I have de-coded the teleprinter read-out does the information really mean anything to me?

If you are unable to answer questions 1 to 6 then as a matter of some urgency take a look at a few good text books. Question 7 may not be dealt with in some of the excellent works on meteorology so here are a few thoughts for you to ponder.

Cloudbase

Assuming the airfield has a good ILS installation most airlines impose a 200ft limit on their pilots. Below that cloudbase they must divert unless the aircraft is fitted with Autoland. In the case of light or general aviation pilots those without an instrument qualification will require a considerably higher ceiling than 200ft. Exactly what the limit should be varies from one country to another. In the UK, for example, pilots with no more than a basic Private Pilot's Licence are not allowed to take off when the cloudbase is less than 1000ft. But suppose that while you are flying there is a weather deterioration at the planned destination and they are reporting cloud at 600ft. What does this mean to you?

Obviously most of the sky is covered in cloud but how about that 600ft? It means that if you are to remain in visual contact with the ground while flying around the circuit the best you can hope for is 500ft ground clearance. The slightest twitch on the elevator will have you up in cloud within a matter of seconds while the 500ft between you and the runway level will rapidly become eroded in the presence of quite minor hills or such man-made hazards as power lines, factory chimneys and so forth. Provided the visibility is good a reasonably experienced pilot should be able to handle the situation; when haze or mist is added to a low ceiling the ability to fly on instruments in answer to radio or radar commands becomes essential. At 500ft agl a 150ft chimney will leave you with 350ft between aircraft hardware and even harder masonry. Think of that 350ft in the hands of a pilot who cannot maintain an accurate height in poor weather and look at these figures:

Rate of descent	Time to descend 350ft
500ft/min	42 sec
750ft/min	28 sec
1000ft/min	21 sec
1250ft/min	16.8 sec
1500ft/min	14 sec
2000ft/min	10.5 sec

Some may regard a 2000ft/min rate of descent as unrealistic. But it is not uncommon for inexperienced pilots, trying to fly on instruments without the necessary skills, to enter descents in excess of that rate. And ten seconds can go by very quickly. Fig. 36 illustrates the point.

In essence you can accept a lower than usual cloudbase provided it is within your competence but the factors that must be borne in mind are:

1.   **Visibility,** since this has a direct effect on your ability to fly with reference to visual cues. It also determines your ability to avoid obstacles.

2.   **Obstacles** within or adjacent to the circuit area.

3.   **Radio aids available** and your ability to use them.

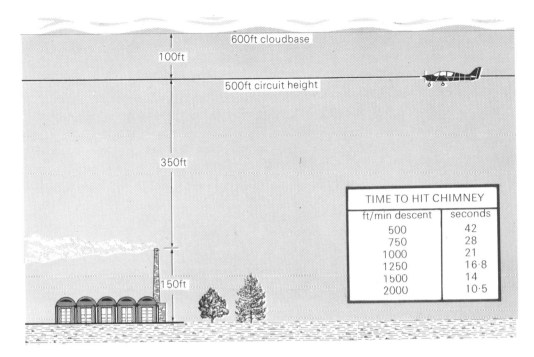

Fig. 36: Hazards of contact flying under a low cloudbase. Figures in the table give the number of seconds before there is a risk of hitting the chimney. Naturally this varies according to rate of descent.

Visibility

Having devoted this book to the cause of professionalism in aviation I have to admit that the professionals of many countries have left us with an untidy situation. It can only be regarded as a prime illustration of the dangers inherent in compromise, because we are stuck with speed in knots, height in feet, weight in kilogrammes and visibility in kilometres. So when the met. man promises a visibility of 2km, a measurement bearing no relationship to the scale on an ASI, an American, Canadian or British pilot usually tells himself 'that's a bit more than two thousand yards' (the South Africans went metric some years ago). In effect 2km is about the length of a good, but not outstanding runway. Most airline pilots are limited by their companies to landing when the runway visual range is no less than 600m (Autoland excepted) but before the approach and landing stage we have to arrive at the destination and pilots without instrument flying capability must find their way by using outside visual references. Of course, visibility limitations are aggravated by aircraft height so we are really interested in *slant* range of vision. In other words at 5000ft agl a visibility of 2km allows one to see little more than half that distance ahead of the aircraft (Fig. 37). From a map reading point of view, assuming you are cruising at 5000ft agl, a visibility of 2km would mean that the maximum distance at which ground features could be seen ahead of the aircraft would be 1295m (4249ft). How much time does that allow before the feature is overflown and out of sight?

Ground speed	Time to fly 1295 metres
110 kt	22.87 sec
130 kt	19.35 sec
150 kt	16.77 sec
170 kt	14.8 sec
190 kt	13.24 sec

When the visibility is down to 1km you will have half as much time to see, identify and overfly pinpoints on the ground. So the simple answer to flying in reduced visibility is slow down to a gallop – unless, of course, you are able to fly on instruments and use the radio aids. When you are flying at 'Low Safe Cruising Speed' visibility ahead of the aircraft may be improved by lowering part flap. There will be a lower nose attitude and the additional power required to overcome drag will improve the effectiveness of the tail surfaces.

Appreciation of forecasts

Carrying the mental picture concept a stage further a talent of great value to any pilot is the ability to read a synoptic chart and understand the various symbols. Features that are of particular importance in the flight planning stage are:

1. **Wind speed and direction** since this affects range and flight time.

2. **Special weather** such as thunderstorms, hail, snow, etc.

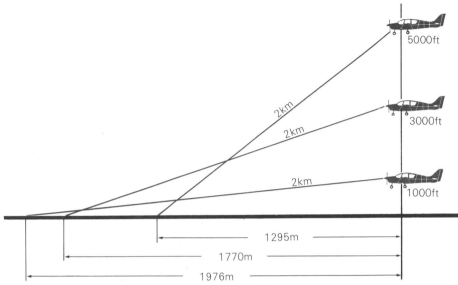

Fig. 37: Effect of height on visual range. (Scale is distorted for the sake of clarity.)

3. **Location and movement of any frontal systems.** Warm front clouds descend and increase in vertical extent as they approach the line drawn on the chart. Furthermore, the nimbostratus clouds which form a line along the front often extend from near ground level up to perhaps 12,000–14,000ft so instrument flying is essential when a warm front cuts across track. Cold fronts are a different matter. They are made up of individual cumulus clouds which extend back from the front for perhaps 50nm or so. In most parts of the world it is possible to fly through the gaps, but at all costs avoid areas where there are thundery conditions.

4. **Temperature and dew point.** Meteorology may be important to mariners but it is vital to pilots – even amateur ones. Paragraph 6 on page 23 explains radiation fog.

5. **Freezing Levels and Icing Index.** This important subject merits a section to itself.

Airframe and engine ice

You can fill an aircraft with every radio aid in the book and get yourself a host of qualifications, but if the airframe has no ice protection it is the height of folly to fly into known icing conditions. If your route involves flying under the rain belt of a warm front and the temperature is at or below freezing watch out – such an environment is ideal for collecting airframe ice. And when you are forced to enter cumulus clouds keep an eye on the outside air temperature. Large raindrops can exist in liquid form even when the temperature is several degrees below freezing. On impact with the leading edges of the flying surfaces the raindrops smear and freeze. The rate of build-up when glazed ice forms in this way is remarkable and highly dangerous because in little more time than it takes to read these words it can alter the airfoil shape to the point where aerodynamics give up and the aircraft becomes a stalled ice cube. Not good at all. The three main types of airframe ice are:

1. **Hoar frost:** This is a thin film of frost that often collects on the airframe when the aircraft has been parked overnight in the open. On the face of it there is not enough ice to have any effect on aircraft performance but it must be cleared from the wings and tail surfaces before starting the engine. Hoar frost can break down laminar airflow and prevent an aircraft from taking off.

2. **Rime ice (Fig. 38):** A white, relatively slow build-up of ice that occurs in layer type clouds. Because air is trapped in the ice it looks for all the world like sugar icing on a birthday cake. If you do not move away from the icing area rime will grow to the point where a flat hammer head of ice will form and that will affect the airflow, possibly to the point where you can no longer maintain control.

3. **Glazed ice (Fig. 39):** As already mentioned this is the product of supercooled water droplets which freeze on impact. The smearing action which is part of the process has the effect of running the build-up back along the wing or tail surface leading edge and this type of

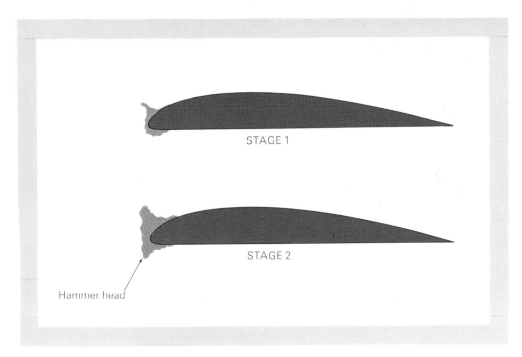

STAGE 1

STAGE 2

Hammer head

Fig. 38: The formation of rime ice. A heavy build-up can destroy the airflow over the flying surfaces.

airframe ice is particularly dangerous to aircraft without suitable protection.

Types of ice protection

The most common method of airframe ice protection takes the form of rubber 'boots' fitted to the leading edges of the wings, tailplane and fin (known as stabilizers in the USA). A sequencing valve induces the boots to inflate then return through vacuum to their normal shape, the action breaking off ice as it forms. The disadvantage of boots is that they have a tendency to reduce cruising speed and therefore range.

Some aircraft are fitted with a porous strip along the leading edges of the flying surfaces through which anti-freeze is pumped. The system works well but it is time-limited by the amount of fluid carried. The idea is therefore to use fluid de-icing or anti-icing to get out of trouble while you

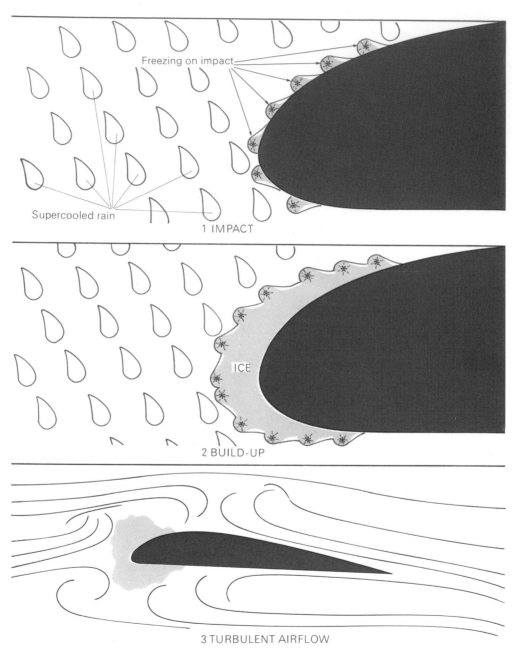

Fig. 39: The formation of glazed ice. Note the smearing action of supercooled raindrops on impact.

are seeking another cruising level where the temperature and humidity conditions do not produce ice. Several forms of propeller de-icing are available.

Most jet aircraft have thermal anti-icing which utilizes heat from the engines – and very good it is too. However, a word of warning about ice protection on light twins. Some of the systems fitted are of the 'Micky Mouse' variety – they will get you out of trouble and no more. For prolonged operation in cold, moist flight conditions you need anti-icing gear that has been cleared for flight into 'known icing conditions'.

Another problem is that of windscreen icing. This can happen when, for example, you have been flying 'VMC on top' and the airframe is at below freezing temperature. Comes the moment to descend through a layer of stratus and the windscreen goes opaque, leaving you to do the landing on the braille system! Large aircraft have electrically heated windscreens, and it is also possible to fit an electric panel to the smaller twins. However, even a modest light single will afford token protection in this area. If you direct all cabin heat to the windscreen through the de-mister it will clear a small patch in the frost and at least allow limited vision out of the aircraft. It is at times like this that a clear vision panel is an advantage.

Pitot/pressure head ice

Very few aircraft are these days without electric heaters for the protection of pitot heads or, when fitted, pressure heads and their related static vents. Unfortunately some pilots forget to switch them on *before* encountering icing conditions and the drama that follows will vary according to aircraft type. Sometimes these vital pieces of airframe, providing as they do a link to the outside world without which the ASI, VSI and altimeter will rapidly go out of business, have been known to collect ice before it becomes evident on the flying surfaces. The loss of dynamic pressure that follows the icing of the pressure tube will cause a gradual reduction in airspeed which in turn will naturally prompt the pilot to lower the nose and so lose height. On the other hand a frozen static source will fix the altimeter and VSI, cause large apparent airspeed increases with loss of height, and, as a result, encourage the pilot to hold up the nose and risk a stall.

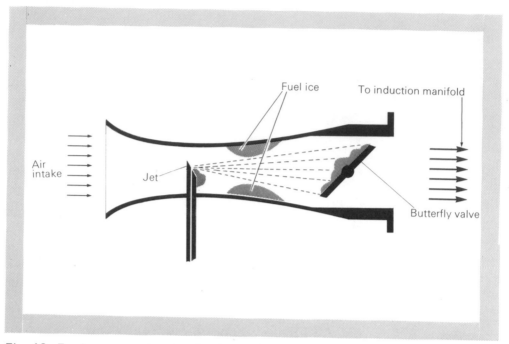

Fig. 40: Fuel evaporation ice in the carburettor.

These are just a few of the symptoms likely to be experienced when the pitot or pressure head has been allowed to collect ice. There are others. But when the ASI hits zero with a decisive clonk don't tell yourself 'we've stopped' but concentrate on flying attitudes with the aid of the Artificial Horizon, the Turn and Slip and the Direction Indicator.

The moral is clear. When the temperature is near or below freezing and moisture is in the air (it need not be cloud, just humidity) then switch on that pitot heater. Because if you do ice up most of them require at least thirty seconds to clear the problem, a period that will feel like thirty minutes until that ASI comes to life again.

Engine ice

When flying in heavy snow, hail or supercooled rain impact ice may build up on the mesh filter protecting the air intake. To cater for this some form of alternative air source is provided and this may be selected by the pilot

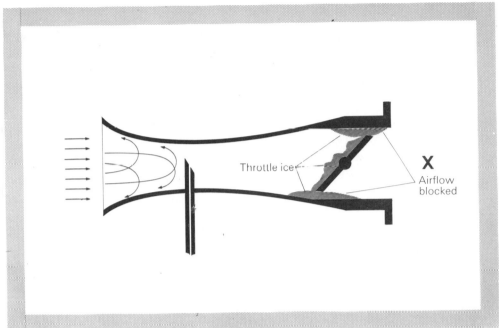

Fig. 41: Throttle ice. In conjunction with fuel evaporation ice (Fig. 40) this can gradually cause a rich mixture cut and stop the engine unless carburettor heat is applied while air can flow through the induction system.

when the need arises. Impact ice is the only icing risk that may afflict fuel injected engines but two further hazards face pilots flying aircraft with carburettor induction:

a) Fuel evaporation ice (Fig. 40): This is caused when the fuel changes from liquid to vapour. In order to vaporize it takes latent heat from the incoming air and the carburettor walls, and thereby produces a major temperature drop within the carburettor. As a result, when sufficient moisture is present, ice will form downstream of the jet. (Compare this process with what happens when you wet your hand and blow on it. Your skin feels cold because the water is taking heat from it in order to vaporize.)

b) Throttle ice (Fig. 41): To assist the fuel out of the jet and turn it into vapour form the pressure is reduced within the carburettor choke (which is, of course, shaped like a venturi tube). This causes the air to expand, so dissipating the amount of heat available and causing a drop in temperature. Obviously the pressure decreases as the throttle is closed – a look at the manifold pressure will confirm that – so throttle ice is most likely to occur at low power settings.

To cater for engine icing in carburettor-type engines the air intake features a valve which, in the COLD position, allows filtered air from the intake in the nose of the aircraft to enter the carburettor. The valve (which is, of course, the other end of the carburettor heat control provided for the pilot) may be closed, at the same time opening a passage through which unfiltered air is passed through a heat exchanger built around one of the exhaust manifolds and then sucked through the carburettor. As every pilot knows the carburettor heat control may be set in any number of inter-mediate positions between its limits of fully cold or fully hot and herein lies the danger. On a very cold day, when the temperature is below that where ice will form, part heat may raise the temperature into the icing range and cause the very problem we are trying to avoid. And the only way to know when the carburettor is in an ice-making mood is if the 'plane has a carb. air temperature gauge.

So in using the carb. heat remember the song made famous by Frank Sinatra – 'All or nothing at all'. If there is a gradual reduction in engine RPM which even full throttle will not rectify, followed by rough running, apply *full* heat. What happens next may urge you to go back into COLD because the hot air of a lower density than before will cause a further drop in RPM. Also ice and water will enter the engine as the heat takes effect – and piston-engines do not like ice or water. However, keep on full heat, give it time to act and make no attempt to go back into cold until the engine is running normally again. Otherwise there will be a 'rich mixture cut', the fire will go out and there will be no heat to allow another attempt at clearing the ice.

It is good airmanship to check for carburettor ice during all flights. Remember there need be no cloud to provoke ice – just high humidity and a temperature of between $-15°C$ (5°F) and $+30°C$ (86°F).

I have dwelt on the subject of ice at some length because most pilots of light aircraft manage to avoid it. Then one day a route forecast says 'icing index high', it is ignored and the evidence has melted away before the true cause of the accident can be established. Some time ago I was in a light single that was leading a tour of twenty-five aircraft. We had been to the Isle of Jerba off the North African coast and the happy band of British, French and German pilots were on their way home. At 8500ft it looked as though we should be well clear of all cloud until, over sunny Tunis of all places, the cumulus started growing quicker than we could climb. At just over 10,000ft we clipped the top of one cloud and immediately caught a packet of glazed ice. Before I could say 'how about descending below the freezing level' the owner of the 'plane, an experienced French friend of mine, was on the way back to 8500ft where the ice melted and we broke out between cloud layers in pleasant flying conditions after no more than twenty minutes' instrument flying.

We had called the others and warned them not to have ideas of out-climbing the now thickening cloud but several pilots ignored our advice. One of the Germans climbed to 14,000ft (without oxygen, by the way) and the next thing we heard was a Mayday telling the world that his engine had given up trying and his instruments were not working. Both problems could have been overcome if only it had been possible to call him up and say 'select HOT air and switch on the pitot heat'. Unfortunately, just after sending the Mayday he went off the air because his aerial iced up. This story has a happy ending because we were later told that, having descended through cloud like a side of frozen beef, he emerged in the clear at 2000ft over the Mediterranean with ice dropping off the wings while the engine slowly got itself wound up again. It could have ended differently.

If there is ice about and the aircraft is not equipped for it you have three options:

1. Continue the flight but climb above the freezing level. Many light aircraft do not have the power to do this and you will, in any case, need oxygen if you have to go above 10,000ft for any length of time.

2. Descend below the freezing level. This is the easiest step to take provided the terrain below will allow.

3. Alter the flight plan and get away from the icing area. This may be your only option. Sad to relate it is an option that has often been ignored at great cost.

Bad weather flying

Heavy rain, hail and snow

Provided the pilot has adequate instrument flying skill the main problems with precipitation are the obvious loss of vision, the need for careful navigation to avoid flying into obstructions and, in the case of rain when the temperature is below freezing, the risk of airframe ice. Besides this, pilots with little instrument flying experience often underestimate the psychological problems of flying through bad weather.

It is quite remarkable how much rain can be tolerated by an aircraft. Speak to any pilot who has had the misfortune to fly through the monsoon over parts of India or the like. The water cascades in sheets yet the engines keep turning while the paint is being stripped off the wings. However, when the forecast says 'continuous heavy rain and $\frac{7}{8}$ cloud at 400ft' be clear about what this means and then be honest with yourself about whether or not you can cope. There is no shame in a little humility, a willingness to acknowledge one's own limitations. On the other hand the big-head who presses on and gets himself in a knot is to be deplored.

Severe turbulence

Above about 2000ft strong winds may not cause much turbulence, the main problem in the case of headwinds being a reduction in range. To the inexperienced pilot the need to allow for 20–30 degrees of drift while flying a relatively slow aircraft in strong winds blowing abeam may come as a surprise. The poor chap may start to distrust his VOR or ADF and get himself lost as a result. When the headwind is such that a revised ETA (based on the known groundspeed) indicates that you will run out of fuel before reaching the destination, divert without delay. It is at times such as this that the importance of having previously calculated the Point of No Return and selected diversions comes into its own. When the panic is

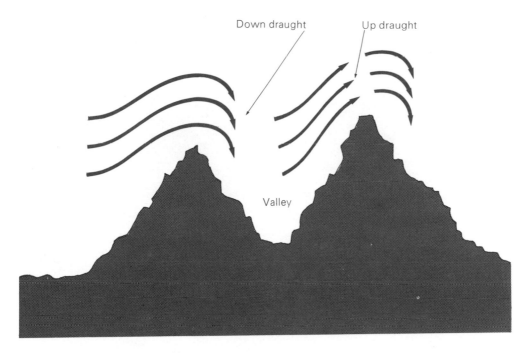

Down draught   Up draught

Valley

Fig. 42: Up and down draughts caused by winds in mountain regions.

on there is no time for the pilot to ask himself 'where shall we go?' or 'have I enough fuel to get back?'

Mountain winds

A combination of mountainous regions and strong winds will produce a pattern of severe up draughts and down draughts and whenever possible such areas should be crossed with a height margin of at least 2000ft. Here are some useful hints:

1. Cross ridges at approximately 45 degrees. If there are powerful down draughts this will enable you to turn into a valley or other area where the ground drops away and so gain vital terrain clearance.

2. Avoid the temptation of pulling up the nose when you experience a

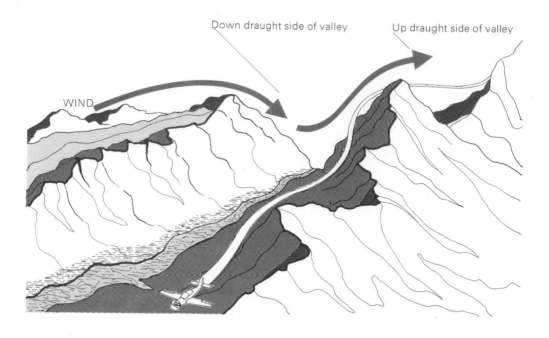

Down draught side of valley

Up draught side of valley

WIND

Fig. 43: Flying along the up draught side of a valley, an important safety precaution during mountain flying.

high rate of sink. Apply climbing power, keep up the speed and steer away from high ground.

3. Down draughts occur as the wind passes over a ridge. On the other side of the valley will be an up draught (see Fig. 42 page 135). Remember this and if necessary turn back, select a different crossing point and make another attempt.

4. If the flight entails following a valley in the presence of a strong beam wind always select the up draught side (Fig. 43).

5. Be on guard for orographic cloud formation caused when the wind ascends the mountains and cools. Such clouds may obscure the higher points which are nonetheless as solid as the rest of the mountain!

6. Before flying over mountainous regions check that all harnesses,

not just those for the crew, are tight, and ensure that all loose articles (briefcases, cameras, etc.) are secure.

Cumulus clouds

Provided they have not grown beyond the 'fair weather' stage, cumulus clouds do no more than cause a little turbulence. However, under certain conditions the little cumulus can grow into a vast cumulonimbus cloud and that is well worth avoiding.

In equatorial regions, where the atmosphere extends to its highest levels, these massive clouds have been known to extend from 1500ft agl to over 40,000ft. They can produce hailstones the size of tennis balls and even in such latitudes as Britain, France and the border between Canada and the USA vertical currents within a developed cell have been measured at 4000ft/min and more. The friction that results from these ascending and descending currents is capable of generating a great deal of electricity and this is stored by the cloud itself which acts as a giant condenser. When the voltage is sufficient a lightning discharge will flash from the cloud to the nearest point of negative potential. This could be another cloud, a tree or, if you are foolish enough to be around, your aircraft.

In theory all parts of the aircraft are supposed to be bonded, i.e. interconnected with bonding wires to provide a continuous electric circuit. However, some light aircraft are not very good in this respect and a lightning strike has been known to remove a wing tip quicker than you can say 'what in hell was that?' Fig. 44 shows just what happens in cumulonimbus clouds and you are strongly advised to give them a wide berth because you risk the following:

1. Violent up and down currents, which can break an overcontrolled aircraft.

2. A lightning strike.

3. Severe glazed icing in regions containing supercooled rain.

4. Severe damage from large hailstones.

5. The possibility of damage to the radio and of the temporary

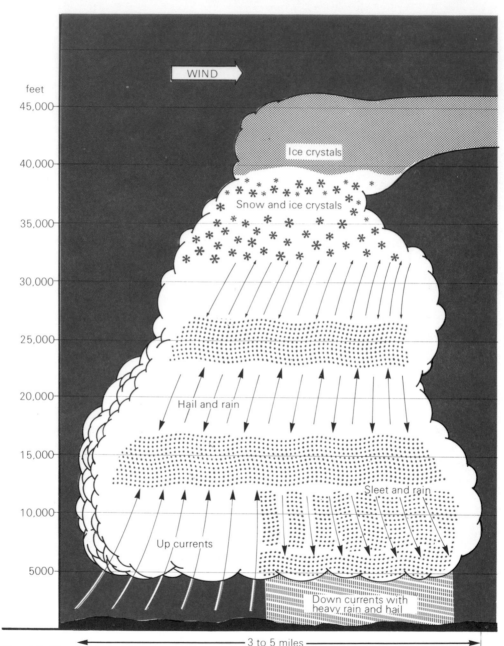

Fig. 44: Typical cumulonimbus cloud in developed state.

unserviceability of the magnetic compass (which will in any case require attention after landing).

It should be remembered that the area for some distance around a large cumulonimbus will be turbulent, and strong vertical currents exist under the cloud itself.

Lowering cloudbase

One of the classic traps of aviation is the lowering cloudbase. The trip starts in reasonable conditions, say, 10km visibility, $\frac{7}{8}$ stratus at 1500ft. Along the route the cloud thickens and its base descends until the pilot, who is committed to maintaining visual contact, is flying in and out of the murk at 600ft. Below there is undulating ground and, at intervals, trees flash by uncomfortably close, only to be blotted out by wisps of low-lying cloud. It is an unhealthy situation, and one that has in it the seeds of disaster. For unless the pilot can see a bright patch of sky ahead he must turn back and fly towards known better weather. Even this action has its hazards because by now the pilot will be in fear of hitting high ground while in the turn.

In most countries the limits for this kind of flying are clearly defined. For example in Britain the authorities require that the aircraft maintain at least 500ft separation from persons or property when flying in open country and the regulations are the same in the USA. So to non-instrument rated pilots the message is quite simply: Do not fly on into a lowering cloudbase if you want to become a veteran pilot. *You have a clear moral duty not to press on in the hope that conditions may improve.*

The instrument rated pilot is able to handle a lowering cloudbase somewhat differently because he may climb into cloud and continue safe flight on instruments so long as:

1. The aircraft does not enter controlled airspace without prior permission.

2. There is no doubt about the aircraft's position relative to high ground. Even experienced pilots have in the past flown into mountains because of navigation errors.

3. Landing conditions are within limits (his own and those of the aircraft) at the destination. If not he must fly to an alternative airfield.

4. The air traffic service is aware of his position so that separation from other aircraft may be assured.

Reduced visibility

Whereas the airline pilot is provided with written weather minima by his company, most private and some general aviation pilots are left to make their own decisions. The first of these is whether or not to take off.

The decision to take off

Assuming that the visibility or runway visual range is within the limits allowed by your licence, these are the factors you will have to take into account before take-off:

1. Your own ability as an instrument pilot.

2. The equipment in the aircraft.

3. The serviceability of the radio equipment and related instruments.

4. Whether or not you will be able to return to the airfield and land safely in the prevailing conditions.

5. Suitable alternative airfields.

On the flight

If, having taken off, you encounter fog or reduced visibility while flying en route these are three possible problem areas.

1. Navigation, which will most likely depend on radio aids.

2. Disorientation, which is best overcome by placing complete trust in the instruments and radio navaids.

3. The risk of engine failure.

Clearly the task of completing a forced landing without power when the final stages entail entering fog is not to be lightly contemplated. Single-engine pilots should therefore not rely on radio navigation to the same extent as their multi-engine brothers. An engine failure in a single turns it into a high-speed glider, and for this reason the pilot should constantly be aware of his position in relation to built-up areas, mountains or other hazards, even when these cannot be seen. In that way he will be able to turn towards more suitable terrain if his only engine stops. Provided the aircraft is turned into wind, is in open country and is trimmed at the lowest safe gliding speed his chances of survival will be good.

During landing

When the reported visibility is less than 2000m only an emergency should induce you to land at an airfield without VDF, radar, ADF, ILS or even a conveniently situated VOR. When one or more of the aids mentioned are provided at the airfield, the minimum visibility acceptable for an approach and landing will depend on the type of radio facility (radar and ILS being the most accurate) and the skill of the pilot. A typical airline minimum would be 600m without Autoland.

Over-confidence has provoked a number of fatal accidents at this stage of the flight. There was the case of a pilot who attempted to land a light twin at an airport where visibility at the time was 100m – one sixth of the minimum laid down for an experienced airline crew flying the best modern equipment. This particular pilot killed himself and three passengers but it need not have happened. Within a few minutes' flying time was a well equipped airport offering 1100m RVR.

One of the traps of landing in reduced visibility is that an airfield clearly seen from above may disappear on the approach because of low-lying fog. Oblique visibility can deteriorate at the very time it is most needed.

Fog at night

The principles of radiation fog (see page 23) should be well known to all pilots and when the ambient temperature is within a few degrees of dew point they should always satisfy themselves that there will be no visibility problems by seeking advice from the local met. man.

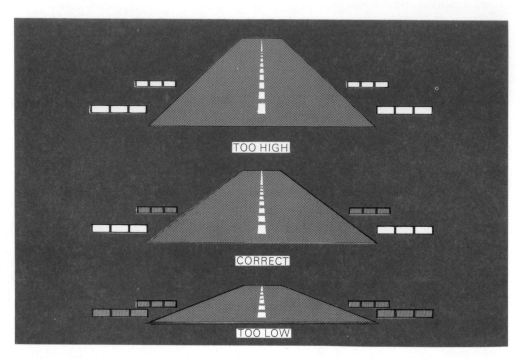

Fig. 45: Visual approach slope indicators (VASI). When all the lights turn red (shaded in the illustration) the aircraft is too low and power must be added immediately.

The risk of disorientation in fog is accentuated at night when the sky is obscured. Lights on the ground may easily be mistaken for stars and this is, without doubt, a time to believe your instruments. Most airports use VASI approach indicators of the type illustrated in Fig. 45 but an improved system, known as Precision Approach Path Indicator (PAPI) is coming into use and it is of particular value while landing in poor visibility. Unlike other approach lights PAPI provides accurate guidance as far as the touchdown point. This is a great advantage because the transition from instruments to visual flight is critical during an instrument approach and landing (Fig. 46).

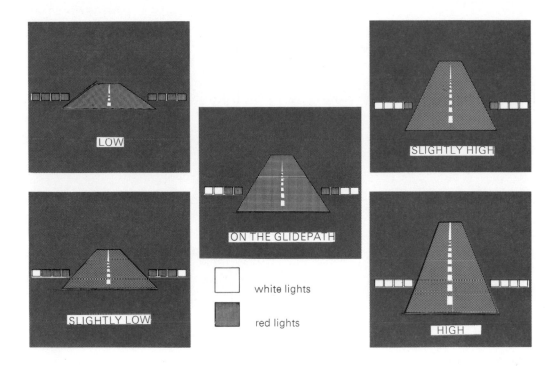

Fig. 46: Precision Approach Path Indicator (PAPI). An accuracy of plus or minus 3ft at the threshold is claimed of these indicators. Transition from white to red is clear without the tendency for white to turn pink that often occurs with VASIs.

Planning a flight in bad weather

Obviously when the weather is poor flight planning is of prime importance. Here are some vital areas that are often overlooked:

1. Be sure your maps and charts are current. Old radio charts may give incorrect radio frequencies and other misleading information.

2. When planning the route take into account restricted, prohibited or danger areas. Avoid obstructions and high ground whenever possible.

3. Unless you are filing an instrument flight plan avoid controlled airspace. Check the latest NOTAMS.

4. Select suitable alternate airfields.

5. For over-water flights carry the appropriate safety equipment.

6. Having obtained a current route forecast and, whenever possible, actual reports for the destination and alternates, take note of the following:
   a) freezing levels and icing index;
   b) cloudbase to be expected;
   c) visibility.

7. Complete all navigation calculations and compute fuel required allowing adequate reserves.

8. Check and re-check all radio frequencies applicable to the flight.

9. File a flight plan even when there is no legal requirement for you to do so.

The modern light aircraft, particularly if it is equipped for flight into known icing conditions, has remarkable ability to cope with poor weather. As always the crucial safety factor is that the 'plane should be flown by a competent pilot. In the wrong hands it is as dangerous as you care to make it. This is borne out by the fact that out of 700 Weather Induced accidents that were recorded over a period in the USA, 341 of the pilots involved had no instrument flying experience.

8. HOW TO COPE WHEN THE ENGINE QUITS

This chapter is devoted to single-engine aircraft, but much of the airmanship described is common to all types of flying.

When you consider the cans in a piston-engine going down under the influence of hot gas, stopping and then coming up the cylinder in an instant, while red-hot valves snap shut behind muscular springs, it seems nothing short of a miracle that it works at all. The fact that a good engine will give reliable service for perhaps 2000 hours before going for re-manufacture is a remarkable example of brilliant engineering and its triumph over a basically crude design.

Without doubt piston-engines, particularly straightforward ones without turbocharges and reduction gears, have become very trustworthy over the years, but even the best of them cannot equal the reliability of a gas turbine motor. We do, therefore, still get the odd case of fuel starvation just after take-off, loss of oil followed by traumatic noises from the bearings, broken valves which drop into the cylinder and do mischief to the hard-working piston or even a cracked crankcase.

There was one widely reported occasion when after the pilot had landed, taxied to the apron and shut down the engine, the propeller suddenly fell off along with a sizeable piece of propshaft; it was funny at the time but could have been a disaster if it had happened in the air. There was an even more remarkable incident many years ago when the late Lindsay Neale, a well known test pilot, elected to deliver a new light 'plane from England to France. With him were his wife and sister-in-law along with two small children. Not long after crossing the English Channel there was a decisive silence from the sharp end. 'We've had engine failure,' proclaimed Lindsay, as though announcing the milk had arrived. This was something of an understatement because at that precise moment the engine, complete with propeller and cowlings, was hurtling towards the green fields of Northern France – having departed the airframe which, by now, was halfway around an unscheduled loop. With great presence of mind Lindsay got the two children into the front of the cabin, thus partially restoring the centre of gravity, and then proceeded to make an immaculate forced landing without power (in the true meaning of the term). Here was a case of a professional faced with the unexpected and handling it to perfection. Think about the situation. Would you have coped? Or can you cross your heart and say 'Yes, I could manage a normal forced landing provided the engine remained in the airframe'? The ability to fly safely in unusual circumstances is only acquired through practice.

In an effort to determine why there were so many stall/spin fatalities we carried out a survey of these accidents and found that it was rarely the man who was practising stalling or spinning at a safe height who bit the dust. It was the pilot under real stress. And when the incident happened near the ground, as it would during a forced landing without power, only the pilots who had conscientiously practised the stall/spin could recover in the limited height available.

The most likely phases of flight when an engine failure may occur are during or immediately after take-off, and en route. (There are not many recorded cases of failure while landing and most of those were the result of running the tanks dry.)

The impossible turn

At Biggin Hill, the famous Battle of Britain airfield not far from London, a four-seat tourer took off one clear day. At around 250ft the engine stopped. Below the aircraft and almost in line with its climb path lay a valley offering the safety of another 150ft and a selection of open fields. Behind, situated on a plateau, was the airfield – one of the busiest in Europe with aircraft taking off in non-stop order. The pilot was known to be a reliable amateur with a fair amount of experience and a balanced disposition, so one would have expected him to make the only possible decision and land down the valley. Instead he elected to turn back, and thus made the gravest error in the book. He actually reached the airfield but the aircraft was running out of speed and height and it spun in within a short distance of the runway, killing the pilot and one passenger and seriously injuring the other two.

One could go on forever quoting similar accidents because they have been with us since the dawn of flight. So many people have been killed while trying to turn back shortly after take-off that most flying training manuals, civil and military (and certainly those of which I am joint author), contain a warning in heavy print which, in essence, says: 'if the donkey up front goes silent after take-off *never* turn back'. So let us take a hard, cold look at what in various aviation magazines I have come to name 'the impossible turn'.

Why not turn back?

Surely, supporters of turning back will tell you, it is better to get back on the airfield rather than risk damaging the aircraft in a ploughed field. And what about the cost and inconvenience of having to dismantle the bird and cart it back to the hangar? So much for brave words. Now look at the facts.

Taking the obvious ones first, there is the hazard of landing in what might be a strong tailwind. Even worse there is the risk of flying into other traffic taking off and climbing out in the opposite direction. But the real obstacle, and a killer it is too, starts long before that 180 degree turn has been completed.

Take a look at Fig. 47 and imagine that you have taken off and settled into the climb when, at 300ft there is a twang and everything goes horribly silent up front. The modern light single tends to climb in a rather steep nose-up attitude and it is essential, immediately on engine failure, to adopt the gliding attitude. However, experiments reveal that when an

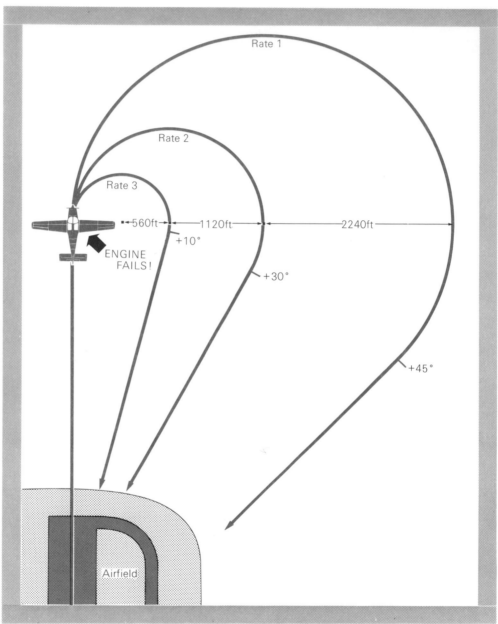

Fig. 47: The impossible turn. Flight path, drawn to scale, of an aircraft attempting to turn back to the airfield following engine failure.

engine fails the average pilot requires at least four seconds to react. Four seconds of sitting there without power, nose held high, will do the airspeed no good at all, so the next and essential reaction will be to stuff down the nose in an attempt to keep flying. At that point you elect to ignore the sound advice in your flying manual about not turning back. Instead you roll on the bank. Remembering the dangers of going into a spin, you start a Rate 1 turn. At the gliding speed of most light singles (say 70 knots) such a turn has a radius of a staggering 2240ft (680m) and, in consequence, by the time you have done an about-turn through 180 degrees the airfield is not ahead – it is almost a mile (1.5km) to one side. (If the radius is 2240ft, the diameter is 4480ft.) Another 45 degrees of turn would no doubt point you at least towards the airfield if not the runway, but then, assuming there is enough height to get back, the landing would be downwind and cross-wind. Remember that a Rate 1 turn capable of heading back to the airfield will be through 180 + 45 = 225 degrees – I shall come back to that later. At this stage critics of the 'never turn back' doctrine are usually quick to say 'forget about Rate 1 turns – get around the corner as if there is a wall ahead'. Well let us study this advice. The following figures, showing increases in stalling speed as angle of bank is steepened, relate to a well known four-seat tourer, one in popular use throughout the world:

Bank angle	Stalling speed	Percentage increase
0°	49 knots	Zero
35°	53 knots	8%
45°	59 knots	20%
60°	71 knots	43%
75°	97 knots	97%

If you do hawk it around the corner on one wing-tip – beware! Stalling speed will almost double. In fact from these figures it seems clear that a 45 degree bank is about the safe limit.

So there you are at rather less than 300ft, starting the turn and full of hope that you will make it back to the airfield. Without an engine everything hinges on *time* – an ingredient so often overlooked by those who favour turning back to the field. The following figures show how long it takes to turn through 180 degrees at Rates 1 to 4. The last two columns on the right indicate how much more you will have to turn in order to reach the airfield and the total time required for such a turn. (All this, with the exception of a Rate 4 turn, is shown in Fig. 47.)

Rate of turn	Time through 180 degrees	Extra degrees required	Total time
1	60 sec	45°	75 sec
2	30 sec	30°	35 sec
3	15 sec	10°	15.8 sec
4	7.5 sec	7°	8 sec

On the face of it a steep turn might seem to be the answer in so far as it gets you round the corner before time dissipates height. However, the drawback is that because of the increase in stalling speed already mentioned, the nose must be lowered to attain more than 100 knots, bringing with it a very high rate of descent.

Let us return to the example in which you were 300ft at the start of a Rate 1 turn. Most light aircraft descend at about 1000ft/min under these circumstances (the descent rate increasing as bank is made steeper). So in this case you have 4 seconds' reaction time plus 75 seconds to turn through 225 degrees making a total of 79 seconds. Translated into height lost at 1000ft/min that means you have descended 1316ft. And, as this little exercise was started at 300ft by now you and your favourite 'plane would in theory be 1016ft *below ground*.

Try the same exercise but this time go for a Rate 3 turn. It so happens that if we allow a little for the steeper turn and glide at 80 knots the angle of bank will be about 45 degrees which, as previously mentioned, is as steep as you can go before the rapidly increasing 'g' forces up the stalling speed to dangerous levels. So we have 4 seconds' reaction time plus the best part of 16 seconds to turn through 190 degrees and point towards the airfield (see table of figures), and that makes a nasty hole in 20 seconds. Even if the rate of descent has not increased during this quite steep gliding turn (and you know that it will) one third of a minute downhill at 1000ft/min means you will descend through 333ft which, even if it is better than the Rate 1 exercise, nevertheless places you 33ft below ground level – and that is before starting the glide back to the airfield. Take my advice and make other arrangements.

Most instructors hesitate to put a figure on the minimum height above ground level at which they would attempt to turn back in the event of engine failure after take-off. There are so many considerations: amount of traffic taking off (you must glide into that and there will be little time to announce your intentions over the radio), wind strength, wind direction (in a crosswind one must make the turn into wind – otherwise its extended radius will have you off the airfield), gliding performance of the aircraft (some are better than others), skill of the pilot (some are certainly better than others) and the terrain ahead. If you are confronted with nothing but trees or a built-up area then, provided there is 600ft minimum between your seat and the ground, there is a fair chance of success provided you start a Rate 3 gliding turn without delay. Even so you would have to face a tricky landing.

By now I hope to have sowed the seeds of doubt in the minds of those who claim that, when the only donkey gives up, they would always try their luck at turning round and going home. When it happens below 600ft agl the numbers refuse to add up.

Engine failure after take-off

On the basis that many an engine failure in the air has its origins on the ground, the best way to avoid such an emergency during and after take-off (surely the worst possible phase of flight for the experience) is to ensure that the aircraft is fit to fly. All the pre-flight checks which I have listed on pages 32 to 38, including the engine run-up, must be completed with care. Power failure occasioned by water in the fuel lines, a common cause of these emergencies, will then be eliminated. (A young student pilot was once asked 'if there is water in the carburettor what would you expect to find in the fuel tank?' 'Goldfish,' he replied.) Likewise if you experience low RPM and unusual vibration during the run-up, and find that operating the mixture control fails to remove suspected oil from the plugs while full carb. heat does not reveal ice, on no account take off in the hope that it may get better. Because if there is a valve or a plug on the way out (or a cylinder head ready to depart) that vibration is likely to become something worse.

Only when you are satisfied that everything is on the top line should you request take-off clearance. Then line up, apply full power and, as soon as direction is assured, quickly scan the engine temperatures, pressures and RPM to confirm that everything is normal and that maximum power is being developed. If there is unusual rough running close the throttle and abandon the take-off; this is no time to be playing the hero. A test pilot friend of mine once said 'many of the pilots I meet are astonished when an engine fails during take-off. I am always surprised when it keeps going.' There is a lot in what he says. After all, it is only when we take things for granted that the unpleasant comes as a surprise.

A blind trust in things mechanical inspires some pilots to switch off the electric pump almost as soon as the wheels have left the ground. The French have a passion for doing this, and indeed recommend it in their flight manuals. The UK authorities have quite rightly insisted on the manufacturers altering their manuals. If the mechanical pump fails and you have switched off the electric one there may be insufficient height for it to save the situation by the time you have noticed the lack of fuel pressure and switched it back on again. So leave the electric fuel pump ON until the top of the climb or at least until 1500ft agl. After all, the only reason they fit an electric pump is to back up the mechanical one in case it ceases to function.

By now you have climbed to 400ft when, without warning, the engine fails:

1. Immediately lower the nose and adopt the gliding attitude.

2. Close the throttle. If the engine bursts into life just as you are well set for a landing in an ideal field it could fail again at the worst possible moment.

3. Look through an arc some 60 degrees either side of the aircraft (Fig. 48). Ahead may be the biggest clump of trees outside the

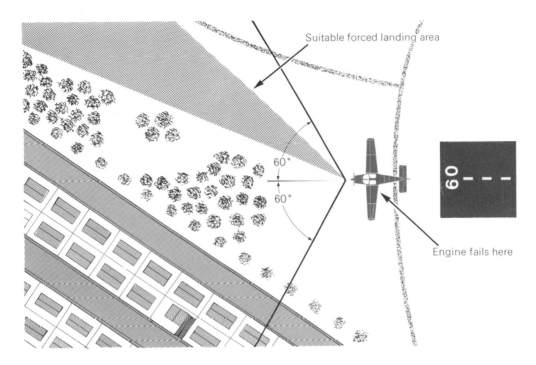

Fig. 48: Landing ahead. Maximum safe heading change following power failure is some 60 degrees left or right of take-off direction. In this case a gentle turn will position the aircraft for a safe landing (shaded area).

Congo. To the right there might be a factory area while on the left is the welcome sight of open fields. Go for them by making a gentle turn.

4. Avoid obstacles.

5. Only if time permits, put out a Mayday and select another fuel tank, but if the engine refuses to run turn off fuel and ignition and operate the idle cut-off. In that way you are minimizing fire risk.

6. When it is certain that you can make the chosen landing area apply the flaps, then turn off the master switch. If you are at risk of over-shooting, sideslip to increase the rate of descent but at all costs prevent the speed from building up. (Check the flight manual.

Sideslips when the flaps are lowered may be prohibited for some aircraft.)

7. Just before touchdown unlatch the cabin door(s). If you do turn over this will help you evacuate the aircraft.

8. *Resist the temptation to turn back and land at the airfield.*

What if there is no escape area and you are surrounded by trees or built-up areas? Turning back will not help because you may spin in at a point that is likely to cause most damage and risk to others, whereas a controlled landing down the best street could have a happy ending. And at the gliding speed of most modern light singles an arrival in the trees need not cause serious injury even if the 'plane is a write-off. Fortunately there are few airfields where aircraft have to take off into impossible situations directly ahead, but in these cases it behoves the pilot to take extra care with his pre-flight and engine checks.

Engine failure en route

There are many considerations that can affect the outcome of a forced landing without power and you may need to take any of the following into account:

1. Is the power failure total or will the engine provide reduced RPM?

2. Does the aircraft have a low gliding speed or will it charge up the selected field like an express train, demolishing hedges and turning cows into instant beef?

3. Is the weather good or are you stuck with poor visibility, low cloud, precipitation, high winds or a little of each?

4. Are you in open country or has the engine let you down over mountains, built-up areas, forest or water?

5. Is it daylight or has dusk arrived, soon to be followed by nightfall?

6. Are you at a safe height at the time of engine failure or is it only a matter of seconds before the ground comes up to meet the aircraft?

7. Are you in the clear, above cloud, or in it and flying on the instruments?

The text which follows will consider each of these points in more detail.

1. Identifying the nature of the failure

While part power may be sufficient to get you away from an inhospitable forced landing area more important to the pilot is an ability to recognize engine failure symptoms. Only then can he try to rectify the situation. Here are a few guidelines.

Symptoms	Possible cause	Remedy
Engine stops running without warning. Propeller windmills noiselessly around.	Check the fuel pressure immediately. If it is at zero, the mechanical pump has failed.	Switch on the electric pump.
Intermittent power loss followed by failure and a windmilling prop.	You have probably run out of fuel.	Select another tank – if there is one!
Vicious shock felt through the airframe accompanied by shotgun-like bangs.	Possibly a magneto has gone out of timing. If left too long this could wreck the engine.	Check each ignition switch and isolate the offending magneto.

Symptoms	Possible cause	Remedy
Decrease in RPM followed by rough running and obvious power loss.	Carburettor ice which, if left, will cause a rich mixture cut and stop the engine.	Apply full carburettor heat, ignore worsening symptoms (see page 132), give it time to work, then, when power is restored, return the carb. heat to COLD but make frequent checks for ice. In extreme icing conditions fly in FULL HOT.
Expensive-sounding metallic noises along with oil leaks and possibly smoke.	There might be a failed thrust race, a con-rod through the crankcase, or innumerable other nasties.	Shut down the engine without delay and hope you have learned how to do a forced landing properly.

2. Gliding speeds

While these do vary, most light singles are usually within the 60–80 knot range. If you plan things properly it should be possible to enter a forced landing area low over the boundary with full flap and at a slow gliding speed, as will be described later.

3. Weather

Obviously bad weather of any kind (rain, snow or reduced visibility) will limit your choice of landing area but, terrain permitting and assuming you have sufficient height to look for a good landing area, more ground will be covered by turning downwind. When they are present it is essential to land into strong winds since these can materially reduce touchdown speeds and thus minimize any damage when the aircraft comes into contact with objects on the ground. Let the airframe take the shock; it will cushion you and the passengers.

4. Terrain

A forced landing in mountains is, of course, a very serious matter but even under these extreme circumstances the pilot can do much to minimize risk of serious injury. In most cases it pays to land in a valley, preferably near a road, but when the ground is undulating aim to land up-hill.

There have been some remarkably successful forced landings in built-up areas but much depends on the availability of open area (parks, football stadiums and main roads). The success or otherwise of such procedures will depend on your ability to position the aircraft for an ideal approach at the correct speed.

A landing in the trees can be accomplished without injury to the occupants provided the aircraft arrives at a low airspeed into wind. When gaps in the wood or forest allow an approach to be made between trees, experience shows that very little shock is felt by the occupants when the aircraft is de-winged. There have been a number of such cases involving even quite large aircraft. A ditching is another matter, and requires knowledge of the sea so that you can assess the effects of the tide, waves and swell. Several text books devote considerable space to the subject and if you do not understand the problems of ditching as a matter of urgency you should read some of them before your next water crossing.

5. Landing in the dark

Obviously a forced landing becomes progressively more difficult as darkness approaches. However, even at night it is possible to land a 'plane after engine failure without anyone being seriously injured. You should put out a Mayday while there is sufficient height for radio reception. In the absence of lighted features such as roads etc., turn into wind, reduce speed to the lowest consistent with safety, switch on the landing light as you near the ground and take gentle avoiding action as the trees or other obstructions appear.

6. Height

Since height means gliding time and that enables you to shop around for the best possible landing area, it follows that the pilot who plans his trip at 6000ft will usually be better off than the ace who suffers an engine failure at 1000ft.

7. Cloud

The main problem associated with engine failure in or above cloud is having to let down into unseen country. Make full use of the radio – if there is a radar service it should be able to guide you away from obstacles such as hills, power lines and lakes. This situation illustrates the importance of knowing your position at all times. When flying in or above cloud single-engine pilots, for whom power failure means going down, should recognize the clear advantages of knowing that unseen below is, for example, a large lake but that to the left is open, forced landing country.

The turn and balance indicator or turn co-ordinator usually works off a separate system to that of the Artificial Horizon, and does not depend on the engine for its power supply. And it is at times such as this that an understanding of flight on the limited panel (page 69) assumes particular value. However, a windmilling propeller will usually ensure sufficient RPM to drive the vacuum pump which supplies the Artificial Horizon, even when the engine has failed.

In conclusion, the two particularly important requirements to remember are:

a) Wind speed and direction.

b) Your position relative to obstructions and ideal forced landing areas.

The forced landing

Although the selection of a suitable landing area according to its colour, appearance and proximity to habitation is dealt with in most flying training manuals, the method of arrival on short finals is by no means standard throughout the world. Americans favour a rather old-fashioned

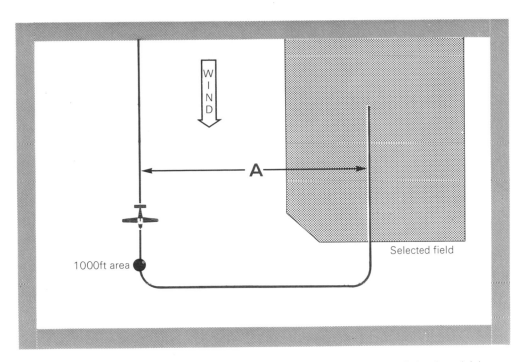

Fig. 49: The thousand-foot area. So often wrongly selected, it should be an airfield width (A) from the landing path and just past the downwind boundary of the selected field.

technique of flying a spiral descent over the chosen landing area while some countries cling to 'S' turns, a practice that went out with steam. The UK Royal Air Force has evolved an ingenious 'constant aspect' system but it is not ideal for high wing aircraft and, in inexperienced hands, the final approach can take the form of a spectacular, fighter-type spiral approach while the poor pilot frantically selects full flap.

The method favoured by many flying training authorities has the merit of simplicity and built-in opportunities for constant adjustment. In essence it involves aiming to fly a near-standard circuit (Fig. 49) starting the downwind leg at 2000ft so as to arrive at the beginning of the base leg 1000ft above ground level. Obviously it is important to have a rough idea of the ground elevation below the aircraft and you should always carry topographical maps as well as radio charts.

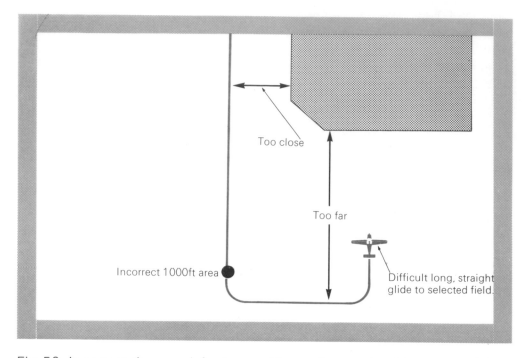

Fig. 50: Incorrect thousand-foot area. Many pilots make this error and find themselves faced with a long, straight glide in to the field. Such an approach is very difficult to judge accurately.

While gliding downwind try to re-start the engine. Check:

Fuel pump ON
Switches ON
Mixture RICH
Change tanks
Carb. heat HOT

and if the engine fails to start put out a Mayday while there is enough height for radio transmission. Then carry out the usual pre-landing vital actions, turning off the fuel and ignition and placing the mixture in idle cut-off. At the same time tighten the harness (crew and passengers). The battery master switch should be left on until the flaps are lowered. When a retractable nosewheel gear is fitted modern thinking is that, if

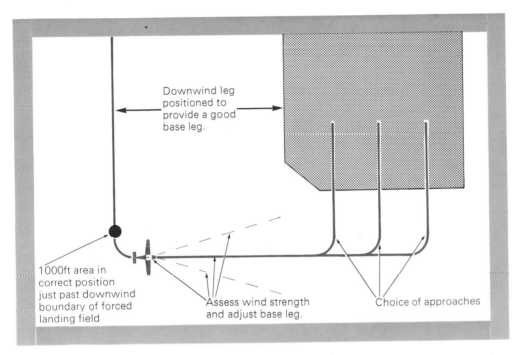

Fig. 51: Keeping the options open. Having selected the correct thousand-foot area this pilot may edge in or out on base leg and turn in towards the field at the best possible moment.

you are landing in a rough field, it should be lowered to protect the occupants from impact.

There are a number of common faults to be mentioned at this stage. First, many pilots tend to position the downwind leg too close for the establishment of a proper base leg. Distance A in Fig. 49 is ideal when the wing tip traces the intended landing path along the ground. Another monumental error, and one that can dash all hope of arriving in the chosen field, is incorrect selection of the 1000ft area, i.e. the start of base leg. Fig. 50 shows that when this is pitched too far downwind and perhaps very close to the landing area the pilot is faced with reduced opportunities for correction. He must turn towards the field at precisely the right moment and carefully judge a long, straight-in approach without power – one of the most difficult tasks in the book.

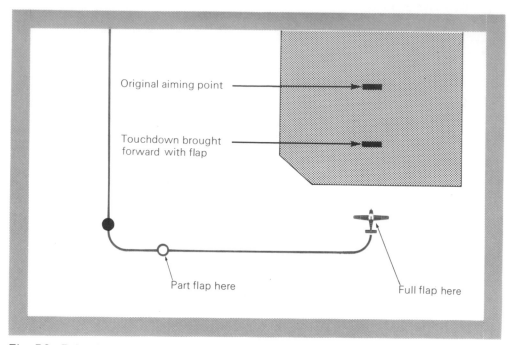

Original aiming point

Touchdown brought
forward with flap

Part flap here

Full flap here

Fig. 52: Bringing the touchdown point forward with flap. You aim to land near the downwind boundary, *not* a third of the way into the field as is so often believed.

Contrast this with Fig. 51 where the pilot is not too far downwind, he has a long base leg in which to assess wind strength by the amount of drift, he can edge in or out to correct for undershoot or overshoot (he could even sideslip away from the field if he was very high), he has several approach options – in fact he has got it made.

The final turn, approach and landing

On the old-established basis that one can always get rid of surplus height but can be in trouble for lack of it, you should aim to overshoot slightly. First select a touchdown point approximately one third of the way into the field. When it becomes certain that you can reach the field bring back the point towards the boundary by applying flap in stages. If it is a small field you cannot afford the luxury of landing too far into the available area. This is illustrated in Fig. 52.

It may be convenient to apply, say, flap 10 degrees on the base leg but it is essential to maintain speed for the final turn. This is the point where the hard-pressed-pilot, his attention riveted on getting into the field, is apt to overcook things and spin in. Having adjusted the touchdown point, the flaps must be fully applied for the landing, unless there is a crosswind. Remember we want the lowest possible touchdown speed.

In the final stages of the approach what looked to be a billiard table at 2000ft will now be revealed with all its blemishes and it may be prudent to take gentle avoiding action when tree stumps, rocks or rabbit holes appear. The landing should be made as slowly as possible, so hold off as long as it will fly, touching down in a near three-point attitude. Take care to avoid any hazards on the ground, and use the brakes to bring the aircraft to a halt, holding the wheel or stick hard back to keep the weight off the nose-wheel. In a rough landing area it may have to take a beating.

On short finals the door(s) should be unlatched and opened just before touchdown as an insurance against being trapped should the aircraft turn over. Having pulled off a perfect forced landing safeguard the air-craft, place someone in charge while you telephone the destination (cows like rudders, by the way) and get yourself a double Scotch.

Practising forced landings

Like most emergencies a forced landing is best dealt with as a drill, and the way to perfect it is through practice. It should be remembered, however, that prolonged gliding, particularly in cold conditions, can very easily turn a practice forced landing into the real thing. So warm the engine at 500ft intervals with the carb. air control in HOT. There is no need to descend until every blade of grass may be counted before applying power and climbing out – across the boundary is low enough. And watch out for power lines!

A forced landing without power may never happen to you. But in case it ever does you should be prepared to come out boss of the situation.

9. BASIC HANDLING FAULTS

What do we mean by handling faults? 'Handling' in the aviation context is a pretty general term embracing use of controls, the order and manner in which they are applied and whether or not they are employed for the correct purpose. For example it is incorrect to turn the aircraft solely with the rudder. The way to ensure a balanced turn is to use the rudder in harmony with the other controls. Correct engine handling is likewise important as it can spell the difference between problem-free running and good fuel economy on the one hand, and high fuel consumption or premature engine replacement on the other.

A pilot who has not developed good handling skills will be at risk whenever he has to face any unusual or stressful situation. He may be able to maintain his skin in one piece as long as everything is going according to plan, but as soon as he is faced with a crisis of any kind his lack of basic skills or his slovenly habits will let him down.

Few pilots are natural born flyers, so what can the rest of us do to ensure that, even under pressure or while otherwise occupied, we can continue to fly the aircraft safely without discomfort to our passengers? The answer, of course, lies in practising good handling and procedures – developing skills just as a musician improves his technique by practising exercises and scales. In order to present what is a very big subject in a logical order I have listed the various weaknesses in natural flying sequence, starting with taxiing.

Taxiing

These comments apply to single and multi-engine pilots. Some of the bad habits described are very common, others more rare but all of them are equally to be avoided.

Moving off without first having a good look around

This can result in hitting all manner of objects from tool boxes to other aircraft and even people. Always have a good look all around before moving off, particularly when you have to emerge from a confined space. Never be too proud to seek the assistance of someone to guide you with hand signals.

Failure to test the brakes

As soon as you have rolled forward a short distance, close the throttle(s) and apply the brakes. If there is another pilot in the right-hand seat get him to test his brakes too, because if he takes over control on the strength of your brake test you may both be in for a nasty surprise if his pedals fail to work.

Turning on one wheel

When manoeuvring in confined spaces it is sometimes tempting to stand on one brake while tightening up a turn. This can lock one wheel, apply severe twisting loads to the affected landing gear strut and damage the tyre. There are, of course, times when it is necessary to make a turn of tight radius and when brake is essential but it should never be used to excess. Short, sharp jabs on one brake will usually help get you around the corner without locking a wheel.

In the case of multi-engine aircraft tight turns are best made by closing the throttle on the inside of the turn, opening the throttle on the outside, applying full nosewheel steering in the required direction and assisting with judicious application of brake. That should get you round the corner

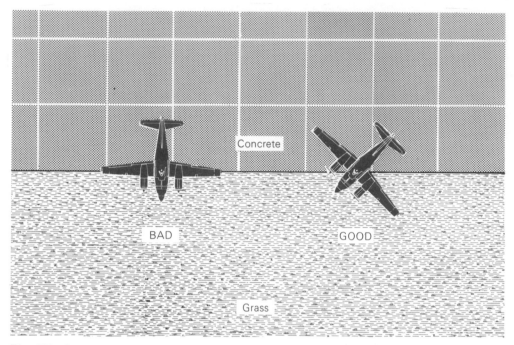

Fig. 53: Correct transition from one surface to another.

without leaving trails of rubber on the taxiway. This technique applies to twin-piston or turboprop aircraft, not rear-engined jets where the motors are too closely spaced to provide asymmetric turning effect on the ground. The latter class of aircraft usually has powered nosewheel steering, a device which greatly assists turning in confined spaces (and demands a third hand to work it during take-off and landing).

Bad transition from concrete to grass

Sometimes it is necessary to park on the grass. When the time comes to move off and aim for the apron or taxiway a concrete edge appears and, unless you know from previous experience that it lies flush with the grass, transition from one surface to the next will mean going up or down a small step. Many pilots disregard the shock that can be produced by even a very small ridge of concrete and press blindly on, attacking the edge with the nosewheel followed by both mainwheels simultaneously.

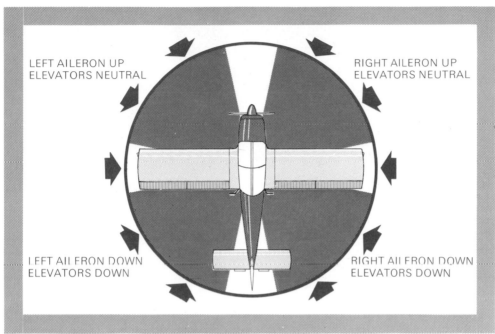

LEFT AILERON UP
ELEVATORS NEUTRAL

RIGHT AILERON UP
ELEVATORS NEUTRAL

LEFT AILERON DOWN
ELEVATORS DOWN

RIGHT AILERON DOWN
ELEVATORS DOWN

Fig. 54: Taxiing. How to hold the controls while ground manoeuvring in a strong wind.

Sometimes the reverse is the case, and you have to clear the apron and park on a grass area that is on a somewhat higher level than the concrete. It is not uncommon to see pilots bulldozing their way into the grass, with the engine screaming and landing gear shuddering under the strain. This is no way to treat decent machinery and Fig. 53 shows that it is better to cross the edge, any edge, at an angle and one wheel at a time.

Finally it should be remembered that most of the small single-engine aircraft with nosewheels have very little propeller clearance and violent pitching of the nose when you are on an uneven ground surface can have the most expensive results.

Incorrect compensation for wind

Modern light aircraft, particularly those with nosewheels, are usually perfectly manageable on the ground in all but very strong winds. Having said this it should not be forgotten that there have been cases when two-

and even four-seat aircraft have blown over while taxiing on very windy days. Possibly the conditions were beyond the aircraft but, even so, correct use of the controls might have prevented what could not fail to be an expensive accident. Few light 'planes enjoy being blown upside down.

Fig. 54 should remind the reader of what control inputs are required while taxiing in a strong wind, but in essence it is all very simple; you move the wheel or stick as shown in the illustration. When the wind blows from ahead of the aircraft there is no need to hold the elevator control fully forward; just forward of neutral will do (remember that tiny prop clearance up front!).

If ever you are caught in conditions on the ground where the aircraft threatens to blow over, do not be too proud to stop and radio for assistance. It is much cheaper to have a man on the wing tip than to employ several in the hangar rebuilding your 'plane.

Taxiing too fast

In the days of tailskids and no brakes, far and away the most difficult part of aviating was taxiing. It did not get much easier when they started fitting those terrible cable-operated drum brakes which faded in use and always let you down when most needed. Along with all but useless brakes came fully castoring tailwheels and then the fun really started – groundlooping had arrived!

The introduction of nosewheel landing gear (championed by the Americans) and disc brakes (championed by the British) took the sting out of taxiing, to the extent that nowadays most aircraft on the ground drive like a car. The trouble with making things easy is that otherwise decent folk are quick to take advantage. The brakes work well, the nosewheel steers without difficulty and they can see ahead, so they open the tap and move down the taxiway as though a checkered flag was about to descend in their honour.

We used to say that taxiing should be done 'at a fast walking pace' and while I would be the first to agree that the modern aircraft is safe on the ground at a faster trot than that (imagine taxiing at a fast walking pace from the passenger area to the holding point at JFK or London Airport!) it should be remembered that even the smallest light 'plane is rather wider than a family car, and if a swing is provoked while taxiing fast, it will rapidly get out of hand. It may even remove the landing gear and cause untold damage. So use discretion, taxi slowly in confined spaces and with caution at all times.

Take-off

Failure to line up on the runway centre

For some reason I have never been able to understand there is a breed of pilot which insists on taking off (and landing) along the edge of the runway. (Given the opportunity, these same aviators delight in starting the take-off from an intersection – thus denying themselves full use of the available run.) Fortunately there is usually someone at the other end of the radio to tell these intrepid aviators that they must begin at the beginning and not half way along the strip.

Taking off and landing down one edge of the runway are activities which are not usually under the control of the Air Traffic boys and are therefore at the discretion of the pilot. They are potentially dangerous because something such as a crosswind or a burst tyre could cause a swing on to the nearest edge, and failure to keep straight during take-off could, at best, have the aircraft on the grass or, at worst, mix it with the approach indicators. By taking off along runway centreline you ensure that left and right of the aircraft is a safe margin, which should prevent you from running into lights or rough ground in the event of a swing developing.

There is another advantage to taking off and landing down the centre of the runway. In poor visibility that series of white dashes flashing by is a reassuring sight.

Misuse of the elevator control

Up in the sharp end of most single-engined aircraft is a heavy lump of ironmongery. Directly below is the nosewheel supported at the end of a long strut. While taxiing, taking off and landing, the nosewheel and its strut take a thorough beating – particularly when the surface is rough. The magnitude of the shocks they receive varies according to the square of the speed. It follows that pilots should do all they can to safeguard the nosewheel by removing from it as much load as possible. The method is quite simple; you hold back on the wheel or stick to raise the nosewheel clear of the ground while taking off.

Judging from the number of collapsed nose-struts that are reported it seems clear that many pilots fail to take this simple precaution. It is particularly important in light aircraft, progressively less so as one graduates on to larger types where powered steering maintains direction until, at around 80–90 knots, the rudder becomes effective. Some pilots even do the opposite and push the control wheel forward which in certain cases, can be positively dangerous. Imagine you are taking off, with the speed building up and everything nice and normal. In an effort to reach a safe lift-off speed you ease the stick or wheel forward. Some aircraft, particularly those with stabilators (known as all-flying tailplanes in the UK), are capable of lifting their mainwheels off the runway, leaving the hardware to run along the ground on its nosewheel. There is an immediate tendency towards the unstable due to torque effect and slipstream over the wing roots and the fin, but it is when there is a crosswind that the fun really starts. Divested of the stability provided by a pair of mainwheels situated behind the centre of gravity the aircraft is now free to pivot around its nosewheel like a dog chasing its tail. This, of course, is our old friend 'wheelbarrowing', a nasty situation in any language. When it happens the first thing to do is to ease the wheel or stick back, so planting the mainwheels firmly on to the runway. If the aircraft is no longer pointing in the right direction, close the throttle before bringing the ironmongery to a halt.

The dangers of taking off in a multi-engine at speeds below V_{mca} have already been explained in Chapter 6 (page 101).

The climb

Apart from the widespread urge on the part of some pilots to switch off the electric fuel pump more or less immediately after lift-off (see page 152) the main weaknesses during the climb are those described here.

Failure to maintain the correct power setting

Unless the engine is turbocharged and there is automatic manifold pressure control there will be a constant decrease in manifold pressure as the aircraft climbs. To compensate for this the throttle should be advanced at frequent intervals to maintain the correct number of inches. Otherwise rate of climb will suffer.

Misuse of cooling flaps

Not all engines have cooling flaps but when they do form part of the kit, use them intelligently. During prolonged climbs on a hot day a glance at the cylinder head temperature will warn you if things are about to go on the boil. If so, open up the cooling flap from its present setting. Otherwise the very high temperature will thin the oil, there will be an alarming drop in oil pressure and you will begin to decide that it is not your day.

Poor speed control

Best rate of climb is usually obtained at an IAS corresponding to best lift/drag angle of attack. When maximum rate of climb is required remember it will only be attained at that speed, and the best way to ensure this is to make full and proper use of the trimmer. Above about 4000–5000ft it is usual to reduce the IAS by one knot per thousand feet but the aircraft manual should quote the correct figure for particular types.

Whatever the type of climb – maximum rate, maximum gradient or optimum cruise climb (the most useful for every day use) – correct speed is critical, particularly when you are flying aircraft of relatively low power.

Inadequate lookout

Even quite low-powered light singles adopt a climbing angle like a home-sick angel, effectively restricting the view ahead. European aircraft offer better forward visibility than most American designs but even in the best of them one can never be certain that the bird is not climbing you into trouble, such as the flight path of another aircraft. You have two options:

a) At intervals lower the nose, have a good look then resume the climb.

b) At intervals gently weave the nose by turning a few degrees left and right of the required climb path.

Of the two I prefer the second method. Unless it is done very gently option a) can generate negative 'g' and passengers find that rather sick-making.

Failure to maintain balance in the climb

It is well known that the only act of aviation charity performed by the propeller is to provide thrust. On the debit side it makes a lot of noise, squanders about 20 per cent of the engine power, gets itself damaged all too easily and, among other undesirable by-products, generates a powerful spiral of air which winds around the fuselage, causing the 'plane to yaw as it strikes the fin. Various cunning devices are employed to cancel slipstream effect but the only one capable of dealing with various power settings is the pilot-adjustable rudder trim. All others can only be fixed to offset slipstream effect at a particular speed and power output.

Some aircraft react more positively than others when the power is adjusted. (The worst I have flown is the old German Fieseler Storch. One only has to look at the throttle for the ball to shoot across the cabin and threaten to abandon ship.) But unless there is an adjustable rudder trim, out-of-balance yaw will be at its worst during the climb when a relatively low airspeed is allied to high power settings.

The amount of rudder required to maintain balanced flight while in the climb varies from type to type but considerable foot pressure may be called for. In the interest of comfort, efficient climb performance, accurate instrument indications and safety (a stall with high power when there is a lot of slip on the balance indicator could be interesting to watch – from the ground), apply rudder in the direction indicated by the ball *and hold it there throughout the climb.*

The cruise

Incorrect transition from climb to cruise

Some people talk about starting to level out 50ft or so before reaching the required cruising level, but this is a hangover from Spitfire and Mustang days when hairy, big-engined fighters went up as if there was no tomorrow.

While such a technique has merit in the case of high-performance piston, turboprop or jet aircraft most of the light, single-engine piston driven tourers climb at rates of 650–1200ft/min and it is better to attain the required level before going into the cruise.

Some pundits recommend climbing to 50ft above the chosen level so that a gentle dive will help accelerate the machinery to cruising speed, but there is little merit in deliberately going up to come down. The most widely accepted levelling off technique is:

1. At the required flight level/altitude, look out and check that it is clear to level off, then lower the nose to the cruising attitude.

2. Leave on climbing power until the speed is near that expected for the cruise.

3. Set up cruising power.

4. Adjust **P**ower, **A**ttitude and **T**rim (our old friend PAT) to achieve the required cruise performance.

Some pilots have the habit of waiting until the required cruising level is reached and then bring back the power while still in the climbing attitude. Then they wonder why height is lost while trying to attain cruising speed.

Flying out of balance

A common fault is to fly one wing low, which is an uncomfortable habit because it inevitably induces a turn and forces the pilot to apply opposite rudder. The cause of this all too widespread bad habit may be:

a) He is gripping the controls with his fist – a technique which on light aircraft is bound to mask all feel and override the trim.

b) Aileron, or rudder trim tabs of the kind that may be adjusted on the ground have been incorrectly set.

To test rudder trim setting you can, in calm conditions, hold the wings level while in the cruise and then remove your feet from the rudder pedals. If the

Believe it or not, the pilot suffered only minor injury following this dramatic arrival. Spin recovery is explained in detail on page 186.

ball moves away from centre, tell an engineer to bend the fix rudder tab in the opposite direction. Ailerons do not normally give much trouble these days.

Fluctuating altitude

Next time you go anywhere with a colleague take an occasional look at the altimeter. Does he fly at or near the planned cruising level or is the big needle in constant motion, fluctuating by plus or minus 300ft? It is a common fault, this business of chasing the altimeter, and usually the cause can be traced to:

a) Incorrect trim.

b) Gripping the controls too tightly so that feel is lost.

c) Wrong power setting.

If you have become used to a particular cruising speed while flying on your own do not expect to maintain it when the other seats are filled. You have two options:

a) Adopt the usual power setting and accept a slight reduction in cruising speed.

b) Increase power to cater for the higher weight of the aircraft.

Unless you acknowledge the marked effect that weight, altitude and temperature can have on cruising performance at any particular power setting, your progress will be on an up-hill-and-down-dale basis.

Turning

Failure to look first

Far and away the most common fault among pilots who are about to turn is failure to look first. High-wing aircraft in particular are very blind while turning, offering little if any pilot vision towards the centre of the turn.

The risks of impulsive action, particularly in areas of heavy air traffic, are positively enormous. That fewer collisions occur than one might expect (having regard to the level of carelessness generally exhibited in this area) is not through any cleverness on the part of pilots; it is simply that the sky is a big place.

Going through the required heading

Often, and certainly when flying an instrument procedure, one is required to alter direction and roll out on a particular heading. Turns on instruments are restricted to a maximum of Rate 1 but when flying VFR a heading change will most likely involve a 'medium turn' which is about Rate 2 or $2\frac{1}{2}$.

Time and again one sees pilots turn until the new heading appears. Then, when it is too late, they roll off the bank, find themselves through the radial or QDM as the case may be and have in consequence to turn back the other way – untidy and counter-productive.

The correct procedure is to start a gentle roll-out some 10 degrees before reaching the new heading when a medium turn is being used, five degrees being sufficient during Rate 1 turns.

Failure to look before rolling out

The same pilots who cannot be bothered to look before turning often fail to check that it is clear to fly ahead at the end of a turn. After all there may be a mammoth thundercloud or even another aircraft in front of where you want to go. So before taking off the bank and continuing the flight on the new heading, look.

Before flight practice

Certain upper air exercises, stalling, spinning and aerobatics (or acrobatics in the USA) involve a loss of height that may be considerable. And while a good pilot will handle his aircraft in a way that does not send loose articles flying about the cabin (negative 'g' manoeuvres excepted) we have all got to learn sometimes and certain precautions have to be taken.

In the interests of safety and other important considerations, various pre-stalling/spinning/aerobatic checks have been devised. The one most widely adopted in the UK was invented by the Royal Air Force and I describe it here because it is the one I favour, although I would not wish to claim that others will not work as well. The main thing is to carry out the checks before you start stalling, spinning or going through your favourite routine of two flick rolls followed by an outside loop and a Cuban Eight. Here is my recommended method. It is named after a nut of a girl called HASEL:

H.	HEIGHT:	Sufficient for the manoeuvre.
A.	AIRFRAME:	Brakes off (some restrict rudder movement), flaps as required.
S.	SECURITY:	Harness tight and hatches locked. No loose articles in the cabin.
E.	ENGINE:	Temperature and pressures normal, fuel pump ON, pitch (when applicable) set to allow use of full throttle, i.e. 2400 RPM for most engines.
L.	LOCATION:	Clear of controlled airspace and not over built-up areas, airfields, etc.
and	LOOKOUT:	Clearing turn to look for other aircraft.

Immediately prior to any manoeuvre that entails closing the throttle, FULL carburettor heat must be selected. In that way its function will be checked. Also if the mixture control is pulled back by mistake this will immediately become apparent as the engine will stop firing.

Stalling

Notwithstanding the provision of elevators that run out of steam at low airspeeds, the impossible angle one has to reach when stalling a modern aircraft and the various stall warning systems featuring bells, wailing

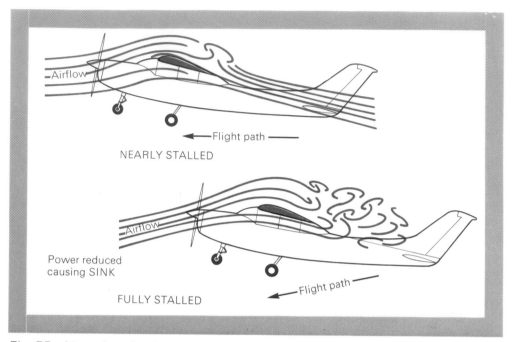

Fig. 55: Aircraft attitude and the stall. The upper aircraft is flying near the stall at a low airspeed. A reduction of power will cause the aircraft to sink (lower picture) when the airflow will approach from below, increase the angle of attach and cause a stall *although aircraft attitude has remained unchanged.*

reeds, horns and flashing lights, people continue to get caught by the stall. Part of the trouble is that pilots will not come to terms with the idea that aircraft attitude is not the only factor. Get yourself flying level at low speed, then reduce power and the aircraft will sink. As it does the relative airflow will come up to meet the wings at an increased angle of attack and when it exceeds 15–16 degrees we have a stall on our hands even though the aircraft is in the level attitude (Fig. 55).

Since you cannot see air flow from the pilot's seat (unless there is an angle of attack indicator fitted on the instrument panel) you are stuck with our old friend the airspeed indicator, a viceless piece of kit that is ever ready to keep us all out of trouble.

Not all aircraft behave like ladies at the stall. Some of them drop a wing in a manner that, if provoked, can lead to a spin. And while modern light aircraft usually carry a pair of ailerons that work quite happily after the stall has occurred, some designs, particularly of older vintage, can become hostile when they are used in this manner. On the basis that in an emergency one should not be having to ask 'can I use aileron on this one?' the standard recovery technique is suitable for all aircraft types, new and old. Here are the main handling faults, but remember that the aim of the exercise is to recover with minimum loss of height.

Incorrect use of elevators and power

If height loss is to be minimized, recovery action must be effected without delay. As soon as the 'g' break occurs:

a) Lower the nose to just below the horizon, and

b) apply full power.

If the stall has been allowed to develop to the point where the nose has dropped well below the horizon there is little point in depressing it still further. Furthermore, application of full power will only have the effect of pulling the aircraft towards the ground. In such cases it is better to:

a) Relax the back pressure on the elevators (it caused the stall in the first place).

b) Add a little power to assist in building up speed.

c) Ease gently out of the dive.

Provided the nose has not been allowed to drop below the horizon before you start recovery action it should be possible to unstall a light aircraft without losing more than 100ft of altitude.

If you do stall while climbing at high power (and, believe it or not, people manage to do that), lower the nose to the level attitude or slightly below the horizon. Full power will already be on.

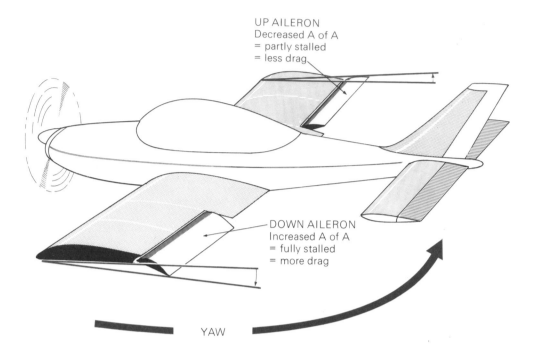

UP AILERON
Decreased A of A
= partly stalled
= less drag

DOWN AILERON
Increased A of A
= fully stalled
= more drag

YAW

Fig. 56: Risks of using aileron to raise a wing at the stall. With some aircraft the down-going aileron can further stall its related wing, increase its drag and start a yaw. All the conditions for a spin are then present.

Incorrect treatment of a wing drop

When a wing drops at the stall, further effects of roll are bound to provoke a yaw in the same direction. At low airspeed this gives us all the ingredients for a spin. When a wing goes down following a stall the natural reaction is to apply opposite aileron. This is safe enough with some types of aircraft but it can be lethal with others.

Take the case of a left wing drop at the stall. Moving the stick or wheel to the right will create a situation where the down-going wing is more fully stalled and the dreaded yaw is encouraged. This is shown in Fig. 56. On some aircraft this action could provoke a spin in no time at all and the correct method of dealing with the problem during recovery is:

1.   When the aircraft stalls lower the nose on or just below the horizon.

2. Apply full power (part power if there is a steep, nose-down attitude).

3. If a wing goes down apply sufficient rudder in the opposite direction to check the yaw. *No attempt should be made to raise the wing with excessive use of rudder.*

4. When flying speed has been regained, resume normal flight and, if necessary, level the wings with ailerons.

Poor lookout

A common tendency among pilots is to complete the HASEL checks I have described and then carry out a long sequence of practice stalls during which the aircraft may cover a considerable distance. It could have moved over a town or airfield, into controlled airspace, or overhead a formation of jet fighters practising a low-level strike! So in between stalling practices don't forget to repeat the 'L' (LOOKOUT and LOCATION) part of the check routine.

Spinning

One of the problems with spinning is that, after all these years of experience and the countless words that have been written on the subject, it remains a closed book to many pilots – an aeronautical exercise surrounded by mystique that is best left to those who are tired of life. In many countries there is no requirement to learn spinning in the course of gaining a pilot's licence. Some places, however, including Britain, have long recognized the value of the exercise.

To this day aircraft are being built that are difficult to spin only when they are flown in the Utility Category, i.e. with just the two front seats occupied. (With this load distribution, the elevators have insufficient power to place the aircraft at a large enough angle of attack for a spin.) But take two friends for a ride in the back seats and this same light 'plane cannot be flown under the terms of its Utility Category, and must now comply with the Normal Category which prohibits spinning. Yet this is the very time, when the centre of gravity has moved back under the weight of those two passengers in the rear, when your docile four-seat tourer will spin like a washing machine. Not only does the rearward shift of the centre of gravity assist the elevators in stalling the wings, it also shortens the moment arm through which the rudder and elevators exert their influence (see Fig. 2 on page 28). And when you want to recover from a spin, intentional or accidental, is no time for a reduction in control authority.

So long as aircraft are capable of spinning, legally or otherwise, pilots who do not understand the correct recovery procedure are at risk. In my view all pilots should be taught the spin and recovery. Whether or not they keep in practice after that is up to them. I have tested many pilots, some of them very experienced, who do not know how to enter a spin. Even more important, they are not sure how to recover! Before explaining the technique, I will give a word of revision on the subject of spinning.

The anatomy of a spin

The sequence of events that can lead to a spin is as follows (read in conjunction with Fig. 57):

1. The aircraft is flying at a low airspeed, say 5 knots above the stall, when rudder is applied (in this case to the left).

2. A yaw results and this in turn causes a roll in the same direction.

3. The up-going wing (right) now collects its airflow at a reduced angle of attack while the down-going (left) one experiences an airflow from below which further increases its angle of attack.

4. At this stage the up-going wing is partly stalled (or it may be fully unstalled) while the down-going wing is fully stalled and the increase in drag that results has the effect of adding to the yaw which started the sequence in the first place.

5. The aircraft is now in a state of equilibrium known as autorotation. This entails movements in all three axes as follows:
   a) The aircraft is yawing (in this case to the left).
   b) The aircraft is rolling in the same direction (in an inverted spin, yaw and roll are in opposite directions to one another).
   c) The aircraft is pitching up relative to the spin axis or the pilot.

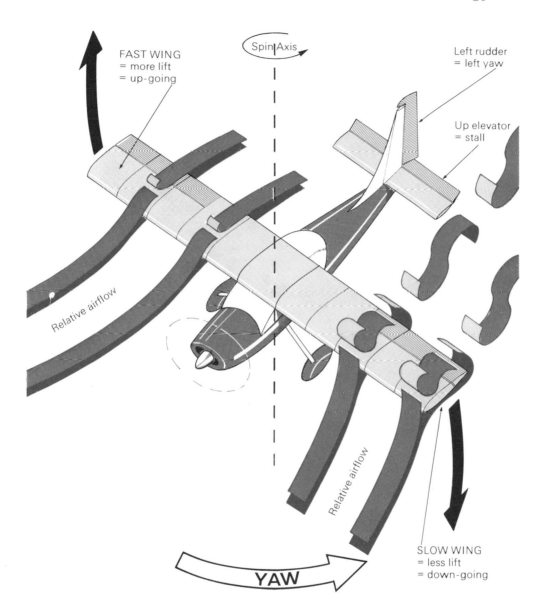

Fig. 57: Aerodynamics of a spin. The up-going wing has a smaller angle of attack than the down-going wing. Consequently it is unstalled or only partly stalled while the other wing is fully stalled, causing additional drag which in turn assists yaw — the cause of the spin in the first place.

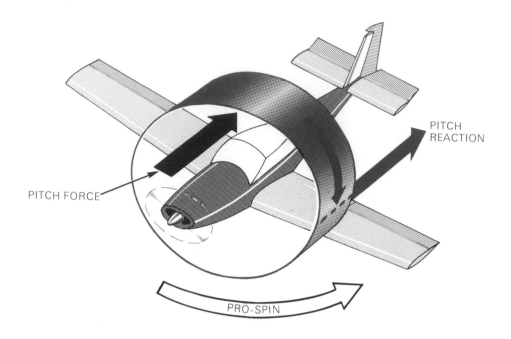

PITCH FORCE

PITCH
REACTION

PRO-SPIN

Fig. 58: Gyroscopic effects of the wings. In a spin the aircraft rolls and the wings act like a flywheel. At the same time there is a nose-up pitch towards the spin axis and this precesses through 90 degrees to cause a pro-spin yaw.

The aircraft will continue to spin (airspeed low and fluctuating about the stall, maximum turn indicated on the needle, opposite skid shown on the balance indicator), until positive recovery action is initiated, and of course it will be rapidly losing height during the manoeuvre.

Why do some spin fast and others slowly?

Without turning this into a paper on aerodynamics I should at least explain that the aerodynamic considerations already outlined are only part of the story. Remember that a large body rotating slowly is like a little one, say a gyroscope, spinning fast. As the wings roll they take on the

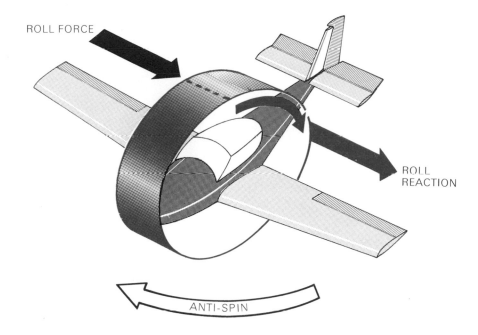

ROLL FORCE

ROLL
REACTION

ANTI-SPIN

Fig. 59: Gyroscopic effects of the fuselage. In a spin the fuselage pitches up towards the spin axis. At the same time the aircraft rolls and this precesses through 90 degrees to cause an anti-spin yaw. The relationship between these two reactions illustrated in this drawing and Fig. 58 (known as the B/A ratio) has an important influence on spin characteristics and ease of recovery.

properties of a large gyroscope (Fig. 58). So the pitch-up movement mentioned earlier takes effect as a force applied to the top of the outsized gyro created by the rolling wing. And being a gyro the force moves through 90 degrees and produces a reaction, in this case on the left. This rather odd property of gyroscopes is known as precession and when it applies to rolling wings on a spinning aircraft the reaction is in the same direction as yaw. In other words it is pro-spin.

Meanwhile the fuselage is pitching up (Fig. 59) and it too becomes an outsized gyroscope. As the wings roll a force is applied at the top of the 'fuselage gyro' which precesses through 90 degrees to become a reaction acting from the rear of the aircraft in a way that is anti-spin.

The relationship between these two reactions is known as the B/A Ratio and on it depends whether or not your 'plane will recover from a spin safely or at all. In practical terms it means this:

1. Aircraft with relatively heavy wings (i.e. large span when compared with the fuselage or multi-engine designs) will spin fast and may prove difficult to recover.

2. Aircraft with little wings and long, heavy fuselages (e.g. modern jet fighters) have a slow rate of spin and should have good recovery properties.

Recovery from the fully developed spin

Since Flight/Owners/Operators Manuals came into fashion, and have assumed an aura of legality as part of the Certificate of Airworthiness, they have increasingly encroached into the pastures of the flying training manual. That would be fine except that sometimes the people writing up advice on spin recovery have never qualified as flying instructors and we end up with all manner of conflicting advice, some of it very odd indeed like 'full rudder in opposite direction to spin'. How do you decide direction – by the roll or the yaw? Remember that in an inverted spin they move in opposite directions. Then some manuals tell you to move the elevators 'half way up'. How can you tell from the cockpit whether they are one-third, half or three-quarters up? One manufacturer tells you to push the stick fully forward (in my experience on that aircraft such action would have you inverted and may even remove the wings), while another advises its customers to hold the stick fully back with no mention of ever getting it forward to unstall the wings.

The problem with these personal methods is that while they *might* work well on one particular type of aircraft, a proliferation of spin recovery techniques is potentially dangerous. Imagine you suddenly find yourself in an uncalled for spin. 'Ah,' you say to yourself, 'am I flying one where we hold the stick back or do I push it forward?' And as you proceed to find out the ground is coming up to meet you.

The spin recovery quoted here is not one invented by me. It is the standard method used by most air forces for basic piston-engine trainers and it is the one expected of UK flying instructors when they present themselves for test. Naturally, the spin will only stop if we can break down the yaw, so to recover:

1. Check the throttle is closed and the ailerons are neutral.

2. Check direction of yaw, if necessary on the turn needle, then apply *full* rudder in the *opposite* direction.

3. Pause for a few seconds (to allow the rudder to bite) then progressively ease forward on the wheel or stick until spinning stops.

4. Centralize the rudder then gently ease out of the dive, levelling the wings with aileron as the speed increases and applying power as the nose comes up on the horizon.

Recovery at the incipient stage

If you were to spin while in the circuit could you recover in time? (Surprisingly enough it can happen, even to the most docile light 'plane.) Try this in a Cessna 150 or 152 – *but do it at 3000 ft or higher*: Reduce speed to around 55–60 knots, lower flap 10 degrees, set about 1500 RPM on the engine and re-trim. Imagine you are descending on the base leg, chatting to your friend in the right-hand seat when suddenly, out of the corner of your left eye you become aware that the runway centreline has been flown through. A bad pilot would attempt to get round the corner quickly and maybe kick on a lot of rudder. Try it. The results can be quite entertaining. For the 150 or 152, surely as docile as they come, will behave like most other aircraft under the same conditions. They will flick into a spin and you will have to be quick about raising the flaps before their limiting speed is exceeded.

Dramatic as this little exercise may seem a good pilot can recover from it without too much loss of height. Incipient spin recovery goes like this:

1. Apply sufficient rudder to check the yaw (i.e. yaw to left, apply right rudder).

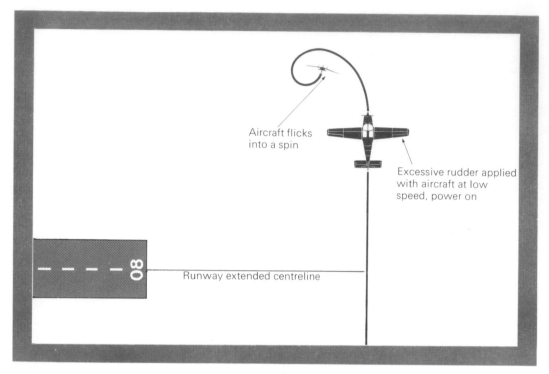

Aircraft flicks
into a spin

Excessive rudder applied
with aircraft at low
speed, power on

Runway extended centreline

Fig. 60: The incipient spin. In this case the pilot has flown through runway extended centreline, tried to rectify the situation by kicking on rudder at low speed and flicked into a spin.

2. At the same time ease forward slightly on the wheel or stick.

3. Provided the nose has not dropped too far below the horizon, assist recovery by adding power – otherwise leave the throttle alone at this stage.

4. As speed increases level the wings with aileron and resume level flight.

The events leading to an incipient spin are illustrated in Fig. 60.

Some old wives' tales about spinning
'You must stall before you can spin'
The rudders on most modern light 'planes run out of power at very low

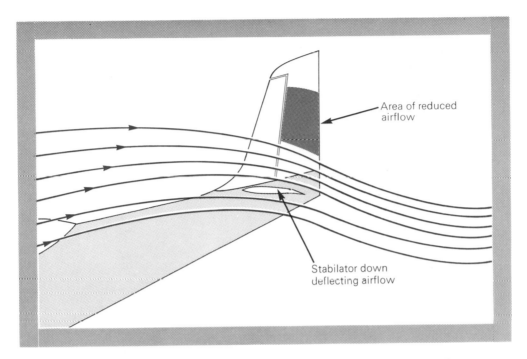

Fig. 61: Rudder shielding effect. When the stabilator is depressed at a large angle, for example during spin recovery, airflow is deflected away from the rudder in some aircraft.

speeds, so if you stall first and then apply rudder the odds are they will refuse to spin. The danger of spinning is that it can happen at a time when you are 5–10 knots above stalling speed.

'Always push the stick fully forward'

This may be necessary in a fully developed spin on some aircraft. But after one or two turns (she may only be certified for up to three) such action could have you half way around an outside loop. Stick to the procedure I have listed, move the stick progressively forward until spinning stops – and no more than that.

'My 'plane doesn't spin'

This is, quite simply, rubbish. I know of one light 'plane that was pronounced 'characteristically unspinnable' by the certifying authorities. We all believed this – until a group of persistent young instructors found a way of doing it that nearly killed one of them. You may fly an aircraft that is *reluctant* to enter a spin. But that is no excuse for not knowing how to recover if it did.

'To recover you just have to push the pole forward'

In some aircraft the action could shield the rudder (Fig.61) and prevent it having the required effect. However, most modern designs would go from a spin into a spiral dive and while one could then recover from that height loss is enormous and there is always a danger of exceeding the V_{ne}.

The descent and approach

The main weaknesses while descending relate to airmanship. It is of prime importance to 'look before you leap'. Never start a descent until you are sure it is all clear below. When descending on the dead side of the field before joining circuit traffic remember it is impossible to see directly below the aircraft (unless there is a hole in the floor). So let down in a descending turn, then cross the upwind end of the runway at circuit height unless otherwise instructed by the tower.

Some time ago a survey of landing techniques was carried out at a busy airfield. Those concerned were surprised at the widely differing standards it revealed. A few arrivals were even regarded as being potentially dangerous. The approach is a critical phase of flight and one where the pilot must be in total command of the aircraft. Too often it is the other way round. Here are some common faults.

Aircraft is ahead of the pilot

To avoid this situation plan in good time. Complete the pre-landing checks well before turning on to base leg. Do not leave the flaps until after the final turn. Set 10 or 15 degrees on the base leg. When the aircraft is of a rapid disposition it may help to lower this first stage while flying downwind.

Closing with other aircraft

Time and again I see a pilot under test entering a busy circuit where there are several aircraft obviously slower than himself ahead and yet he makes no attempt to space himself out. He would if we were in his car but not in a 'plane. We therefore bunch up on the approach, with sweat pouring and eyes twitching, and finally have to go round again. Surely a little common sense demands that when you see another aircraft ahead, you should slow down.

Bad final turn

The problems of turning on to the approach in a crosswind were discussed on page 89 and illustrated in Fig. 28. Even when the wind blows down the runway some pilots have a talent for flying through the extended centreline. Usually this is because the downwind leg is too close to the airfield, consequently the base leg is curtailed and the aircraft is ahead of the pilot. So give yourself room on the circuit and aim to make a wide, sweeping turn on to finals rather than a steep one of tight radius.

Poor speed control

An approach at low speed in the wrong hands can be potentially dangerous but excessive speed may, under some conditions, result in running out of runway. Learn the correct approach speeds for various conditions and use the trimmer to attain them.

Incorrect use of throttle (Fig. 62)

While 'elevator controls height; power controls speed' works nicely with most jets, the good old fashioned 'speed with elevators; height with power' concept is better for piston-engine aircraft. Poor glide path control is sometimes the result of confusion over which control is responsible for what, but the most common cause is lack of reference point. Find something on the windscreen to line up with the runway threshold, then:

1.   Aim to keep the picture static.

2.   If the threshold starts to move *down* the windscreen and the runway

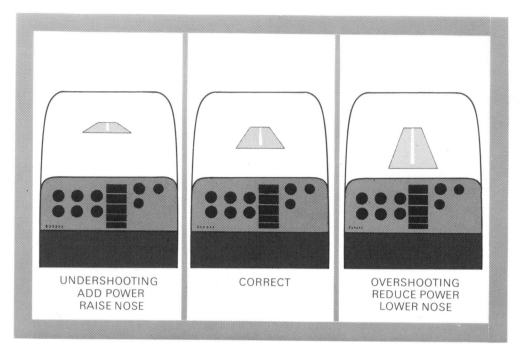

UNDERSHOOTING ADD POWER RAISE NOSE	CORRECT	OVERSHOOTING REDUCE POWER LOWER NOSE

Fig. 62: Adjusting the approach. Prime cue is the position of the runway threshold on the windscreen. Additional visual reference is provided by the aspect of the runway (i.e. flat or standing on end).

begins to stand on end you are overshooting, so reduce power a little and lower the nose slightly to maintain a constant speed.

3.   If the threshold starts to move *up* the windscreen and the runway begins to flatten in perspective you are undershooting, so add a little power and raise the nose slightly to maintain a constant airspeed.

In this way it is possible to fly a very accurate approach path and land at a point of your own choice – not wherever the aircraft wants to take you!

Incorrect use of flap
This topic was dealt with in connection with short field operations on page 52, but misuse of flap is common among pilots landing at any airfield. Main faults are:

1. Some people are reluctant to use full flap, so the aircraft floats down the runway and is never under full control of the pilot.

2. When full flap is used, some pilots apply them in one selection, usually on the base leg.

A guiding principle of pilot skill has always been smooth transition from one mode of flight to the next. Flaps on some aircraft of old design were either up or down. These days it is recognized that flaps should be adjusted to the requirements of the moment – 10–15 degrees downwind to give better control and an improved view ahead while flying at reduced speed, half flap for the approach so that power may be used to control the rate of descent to fine limits, etc.

The disadvantages of applying full flap too soon are:

a) Thrashing in on the approach, mile after mile of high engine power battling against maximum drag, is a pointless exercise.

b) If, for any reason, it is necessary to initiate overshoot action it is better to do so from a position of part, rather than full flap. In most aircraft trim changes are less and there is little tendency to sink when only part flap has to be retracted.

On short finals, when you are committed to the landing and it is safe to do so apply *full* flap. Only then will the aircraft be correctly set up for the best transition from air to ground. At this stage of the approach the strength of the wind should not affect the decision to use full flap, and only if there is a crosswind should you decide to limit their use to about half (or as recommended in the aircraft manual).

Incorrect final approach speed

An engine-assisted approach is easier to judge than a glide approach because the pilot is able to vary the rate of sink with one hand while he controls speed with the other. For this advantage to be fully effective a speed rather lower than that for best gliding performance must be used in the final stages of the approach. Only then will the pilot have available to him a useful rate of sink when power is reduced to correct an approach that is too high.

Poor approach path

Common faults during the approach are:

1. Long, low drag in with too much power, restricted view ahead and poor obstacle clearance.

2. High, near-overshoot dive attack on the runway, power off, followed by a high-speed float across the ground and an arrival that often terminates in a smell of burning rubber.

A 3 degree 'glide path' is ideal and as a guide these figures may help you to check progress:

Distance from threshold	Height above airfield
4nm	1250ft
3nm	950ft
2nm	650ft
1nm	350ft
$\frac{1}{2}$nm	190ft

The height figures allow about 30ft for crossing the end of the runway.

Landing

One would have thought that the introduction of nosewheels should have greatly reduced the number of landing accidents. After all, aircraft with the third wheel at the front are far easier to land than taildraggers. Yet almost every accident summary lists enough busted nosewheels, mangled props and shockloaded engines to start a breaker's yard. Possibly it is because nosewheel aircraft have taken much of the skill out of landing and so people have come to expect the impossible. One even meets instructors

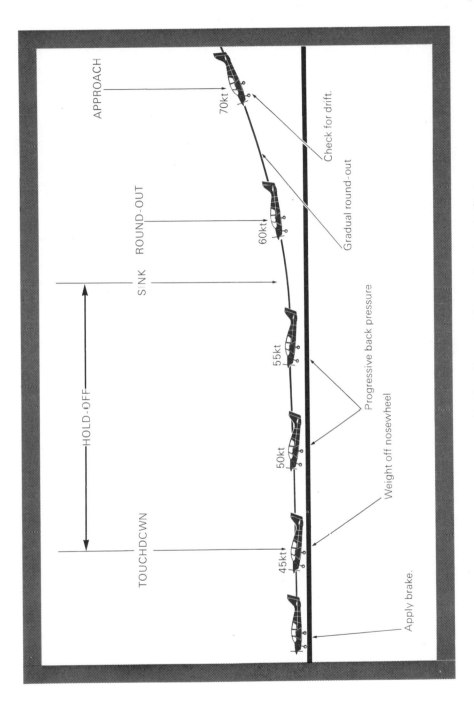

Fig. 63: The correct landing sequence. By landing on the mainwheels first there is a low touchdown speed, no risk of wheelbarrowing and less strain on the nosewheel strut.

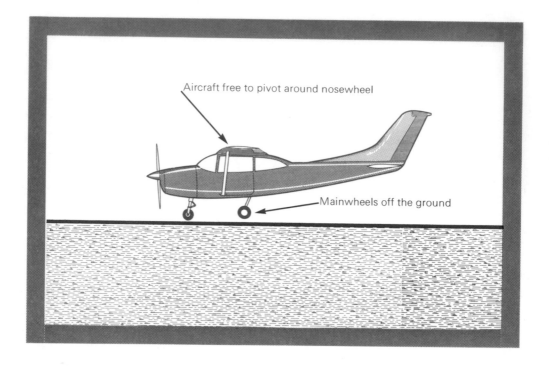

Aircraft free to pivot around nosewheel

Mainwheels off the ground

Fig. 64: The dangers of wheelbarrowing. With the mainwheels off the runway a combination of torque, slipstream and crosswind can cause the aircraft to pivot around its nosewheel when the centre of gravity will take over and produce a situation that is difficult or even impossible to control.

who land with all wheels touching the ground simultaneously or occasionally nosewheel first. And if these instructors are so bad at landing who can expect their students to know better?

Nosewheel or not, the need to 'hold off' during the landing still remains and it is because this has become a lost art that there are so many damaged nosestruts. The aim should be to land in a tail-down attitude, maintain back pressure on the wheel or stick and allow the nosewheel to make gentle contact with the runway. Only then is it safe to use the brakes. The correct landing sequence is illustrated in Fig. 63. Note that power is left on until after the round-out.

The dangers of not holding off during the landing are:

a) Touchdown speed is needlessly high, causing unnecessary wear to tyres, brakes and all parts of the landing gear.

b) There is the risk of landing nosewheel first, bringing with it the possibility of wheelbarrowing (explained on page 95 and illustrated in Fig. 64).

The bad habits listed in this chapter are those most frequently exhibited by private and some general aviation pilots. No doubt there are a few others around. If only some, not even all, of the poor techniques I have described, could be improved the number of accidents would be greatly reduced.

10. SEAPLANE SAFEGUARDS

There are, of course, plenty of opportunities in landplane flying for the unwary to get themselves into trouble, but if good airmanship is essential for the safety of landplane pilots, that in itself will not suffice for anyone who decides to go seaplane flying. He, in addition, must develop good seamanship. The study of tides, wave forms, swells etc. is an important subject in its own right and pilots wishing to become involved in the fascinating art of seaplane flying are strongly advised to read all they can on the subject. This chapter is devoted to some of the traps that await the inexperienced or those who feel that as landplane drivers they have little to learn about floatplanes or flying boats.

The two basic facts to remember about seaplanes are, first, that they have no brakes, which is unfortunate because they are affected by both wind and current while on the water. When the engine is stopped or idling there is a natural tendency for them to weathercock into wind and this should not be overlooked while you are manoeuvring in confined spaces. The second point to remember is that in the air floatplanes handle rather poorly compared with their landplane counterparts. The weight of the floats, their keel area and additional drag all have an adverse effect on rate of climb, cruising speed, ceiling, glide performance and useful load.

Preparation before flight

In addition to all the usual pre-flight checks here are a few more that apply to seaplanes.

Checking the floats

In varying degrees most floats leak, particularly those that have suffered heavy landings. It is therefore important to check the bilges and, if necessary, pump them out. Remember that any unwanted water will add considerably to the weight of the aircraft. In itself that is bad enough, but if in addition all the surplus weight is confined to one float there will be a tendency for the floatplane to execute an involuntary slow roll immediately after taking off. Another hazard is presented when water is confined to the front or rear compartments of the floats, as this can seriously affect the position of the centre of gravity.

Suitable footwear

Shoes with nails or irons on the heels and soles can seriously damage the upper surfaces of floats. Ideally crew and passengers should wear footwear with soft soles capable of providing a good grip in wet conditions.

Minimum equipment

Before starting a flight the following equipment should be checked on board and securely stowed:

a) A suitable filter (e.g. chamois leather) for use when refuelling from cans.

b) Bilge pump.

c) Paddles.

d) Lifejackets for all occupants. These should be worn, or else stowed in a readily accessible position.

e) Suitable mooring lines. These should be at least 25ft (8m) long.

f) Anchor complete with a 50ft (15m) line.

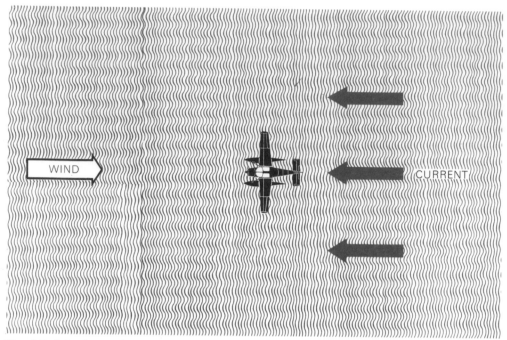

Fig. 65: Ideal conditions for a seaplane take-off.

State of the water

Currents become significant when they exceed about 5 knots and a strong current running in the same direction as the wind can make manoeuvring on water difficult, particularly when you are mooring in confined spaces. Ideal current and wind conditions for seaplane operations are:

    a) During take-off: Into wind with a following current (Fig. 65).
    b) While alighting: Into wind and into current (Fig. 66).

Assessing the state of the water demands considerable experience and skill. For example the flight manual may advise that the maximum wave height for safe operation is 12in (300mm), but judging the exact height of a wave is not easy. In general terms, when the floats span less than two and a half waves along their length the wave formation has grown beyond safe limits for that seaplane.

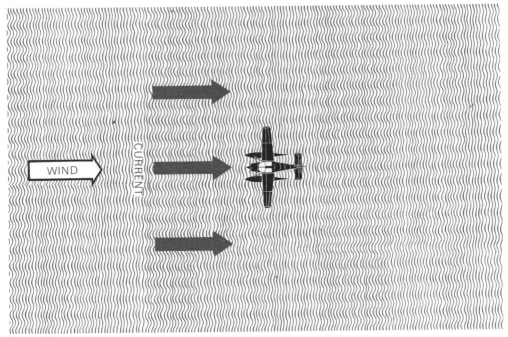

Fig. 66: Ideal conditions for an alighting seaplane.

While operating off the sea or large lakes pilots must, on occasions, take account of the swell. This will often bear no relationship to the general wave formation but there are very real dangers to ploughing into a swell during take-off or while alighting.

Debris

Before alighting on a strange area of water it is good practice to fly over at reduced speed and a low height. Aim to fly to the right of the intended alighting path so that you can see the surface by looking out to the left. While carrying out the inspection it should be possible to select a suitable taxi route that is free from obstructions.

It is good practice to taxi the length of the intended run before take-off. In that way swimmers and debris on (or just below) the surface can be seen and avoided.

Mooring and casting off

If you have to tie up single-handed you need a certain amount of agility. One or two of the seaplane training manuals make it sound very much like a description of where the film star hands over to the stunt man. They talk of shutting down the engine and leaving the cabin to stand on a float before jumping on to the jetty, rope in hand, as the seaplane is wafted by on the local current or a gentle breeze. Naturally such a performance demands nice timing (and considerable confidence if, like me, one is not a good swimmer). It is also essential to ensure, when you jump off with the mooring rope, that the other end is secured to the seaplane – a little detail calculated to save you the considerable anguish of watching your favourite seaplane drift across the lake and on to the rocks while you stand on the jetty with a useless coil of rope in your hand!

When tying up to a jetty, stage or buoy remember that the seaplane has a natural tendency to ride into wind. Be sure therefore that if the wind direction changes it will not move the aircraft into contact with over-hanging branches, rocks, boats or other objects.

Before you cast off it is vital to assess the wind and be in no doubt about the line of drift that will occur when the seaplane is freed of its moorings. Wind, current and the amount of open water available for manoeuvring must all be taken into account before you make a decision on the following important matters:

a) Whether or not the engine should be started before casting off.

b) Whether to move away from the mooring nose first, tail first or possibly sideways under the influence of wind and current.

A word of warning about boarding seaplanes that are moored to buoys: It is possible that the aircraft may be floating directly above a substantial anchor point. If the water is low the act of standing on a float could bring it down on to the anchor point and cause serious damage below the water-line.

A tranquil picture, and a reminder that after alighting on the water a seaplane becomes a boat. The pilot must then exercise skills of seamanship along with those of airmanship.

Taxiing on the water

The recognized methods of taxiing are sailing, idling, nose-up taxiing and step taxiing. On the assumption that readers of this chapter are already seaplane pilots I will not describe these techniques but merely mention some of the pitfalls.

Sailing

Used on its own or in conjunction with idling this is a useful and widely adopted method of getting across the water. However, a word of warning here. When sailing in the presence of obstacles you must be absolutely certain that wind and current will carry the seaplane in a safe direction. Unless you know that the engine starts easily, avoid sailing in close proximity to obstacles with the motor switched off.

Idling

The water rudders are at their most effective at the speed achieved by most seaplanes with their engine idling (about 7 knots).

A common fault among pilots is to ignore the extensive damage caused to the propeller by spray. The only way to minimize this is to taxi with the stick or wheel held back, in an effort to ensure maximum propeller clearance from the water.

When taxiing crosswind, either sailing or idling, the stick or wheel must be held towards the wind, so preventing a wing from rising.

Nose-up taxiing

This method is best left to experienced marine aviators. The technique, which involves using about 50 per cent engine power with the stick or wheel held fully back, is adopted when high winds prevent you from turning downwind using the idling method. In general, if the wind is strong enough to demand use of the nose-up mode, inexperienced seaplane pilots should not be flying.

A similar method is, of course, used for the run-up but the disadvantages of nose-up taxiing are as follows:

a) Because of the high nose angle the view ahead is very restricted.

b) The engine is at relatively high power at a time when the seaplane is moving along the water at low speed, consequently there is a danger that the engine will overheat. At intervals check the cylinder head temperature gauge.

c) The floats have most of their side area ahead of the centre of buoyancy, consequently when taxiing nose-up in a strong crosswind there is a marked tendency to weathercock downwind (i.e. contrary to the usual seaplane habit of naturally heading into wind).

Step taxiing

This is the most rapid way of moving across the water. It entails planing on the step at speed while using about 65 per cent power, and should be used with discretion. Here are some of the things to watch:

a) The water rudders must be retracted.

b) If the stick is held too far forward, porpoising will result. On no account should this be allowed to develop as the results can be catastrophic. Provided porpoising is recognized and dealt with immediately the remedy is simply a matter of moving the stick or wheel back slightly. When it has been allowed to develop, the throttle must be closed and the stick or wheel brought fully back to get the seaplane off the step and into full buoyancy.

c) Speed during step taxiing is likely to be in excess of 25 knots and particular care must be exercised while turning. There is a tendency for the aircraft to lean away from the turn causing one float to be pressed further into the water than the other. In the case of amphibians or flying boats the wing tip float on the outside of the turn will likewise be forced deeper into the water than that on the inside of the turn. A wave or swell might further lift the float already partly out of the water and it only requires a strong enough crosswind under the raised wing for the seaplane to capsize.

The utmost care must be exercised when turning on the step – unless you particularly enjoy swimming away from a rapidly sinking seaplane!

Taking off

One should never underestimate the amount of room that will be required to take off and climb away safely. When the wind is either very strong or dead calm, conditions are obvious but it is the intermediate, moderate-strength wind that can catch the unwary and lull him into believing there is plenty of take-off run available. Here are some thoughts for special consideration:

1. The stick or wheel must be held fully back before you open the throttle in order to safeguard the propeller from the damaging effect of spray.

2. Part of the vital actions when flying amphibians is to check that the wheels are up. It is important not to forget this because the trip may have started by running down a ramp or beach and self-launching into the water.

3. In conditions of little or no wind special care must be exercised, particularly when the surface is glassy.
   Problems arise, because:

   a) lack of wind requires the seaplane to reach a higher than usual water speed before lift-off and water drag will be very high as a result.

   b) Glassy water tends to stick to the hull or floats, so resisting take-off. This stickiness may be overcome by rocking the wings in the case of floatplanes although the technique is less effective with flying boats or amphibians. Probably a better procedure is to roughen the water beforehand by nose-up taxiing down the take-off path. Another rocking method sometimes used to induce a reluctant seaplane on to the step is a form of controlled por-

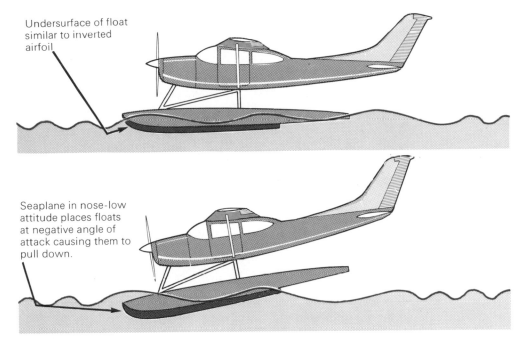

Undersurface of float similar to inverted airfoil

Seaplane in nose-low attitude places floats at negative angle of attack causing them to pull down.

Fig. 67: Reverse camber effect of floats. When the bows are low in the water and the seaplane is moving at speed (i.e. with the aircraft in a tail-high attitude) the under surface of the floats can act as an inverted airfoil and cause the situation illustrated in the lower picture.

poising generated by moving the stick or wheel back and forth, but when a combination of no wind, glassy water and a high temperature makes it difficult to take off it is better to wait for a breeze or, if possible, reduce the load being carried.

c) There is a temptation to pull the aircraft off the water but this brings with it the risk of dragging the heel of the hull or floats, a characteristic known as 'skipping' which is similar to mild porpoising.

d) Because of the high water speed when taking off in a flat calm there is a danger that the floats may tend to pull down. In effect the understide of the float or hull is shaped like an inverted airfoil and if the forward portion is allowed to make contact with the water while take-off power is applied, violent porpoising may occur (Fig. 67).

Immediately after take-off

It is very important not to begin the climb away until you have reached a safe speed. Never forget that:

1. Floatplanes glide like a winged brick and must attain a steep, nose-down attitude if they are to maintain a safe speed for an engine-off landing. This speed must be at least 10 knots above that for a normal powered approach. So if the engine fails at a time when your floatplane is climbing nose-high with its airspeed dangerously low, the transition from steep nose-up to steep nose-down is going to entail a decisive loss of height followed by a heavy landing.

2. Light amphibians have a special problem because the engine and propeller are situated high up above the drag vector. Add power and there is a nose-down trim change but when the engine fails the nose will rise unless it is firmly prevented by a determined pilot. The hazards of climbing away at a dangerously low airspeed, compounded by risk of the nose shooting up in the event of a power failure, should now be clear.

So whether you are flying a floatplane or an amphibian/flying boat the message has got to be – immediately after lift-off build up plenty of speed by holding the aircraft parallel to the surface. Only then is it safe to climb away.

Alighting on the water

The biggest problem facing the seaplane pilot about to alight is the constantly changing nature of the water. Not only is it affected by the wind but past disturbances, particularly at sea or on very large lakes, create a swell motion that may act in a different direction to the wave pattern.

Possibly the greatest hazard to floatplanes and small flying boats or amphibians is the possibility of landing into the rising face of a swell. Water at speed, or when opposing a fast-moving boat or seaplane, can be remarkably unyielding and very severe damage may be caused to the seaplane that arrives on or into the rising face of a swell.

While it is best to plan to alight into wind, when a swell is running this must take precedent and the touchdown should be parallel to the trough pattern, if possible on a crest. Other aspects of the water that must be taken into account are:

a) Position of boats and other seaplanes.

b) Possibility of swimmers in the alighting area.

c) Floating or submerged debris.

d) Large flocks of birds that may rise into the path of the aircraft in the final stages of the approach.

The 'dummy run' mentioned on page 201 should enable you to assess the four potential hazards listed here.

Determining wind direction

In the absence of smoke indications there are others available to you. Birds always alight into wind and, if the breeze is strong enough, moored boats point towards it in much the same manner as a weathercock. When there are no obliging birds or parked boats, wind lanes may be discernable on the surface. If there is sufficient wind to cause white-caps on the wave pattern these are a good indication, but beware – the streaks of foam appear to blow *into* wind. This, of course, is an illusion caused by the fact that the waves are moving back under the foam.

Alighting

The technique of alighting on the water and the special procedure to adopt when glassy conditions make it difficult or impossible to recognize the surface will be known to all seaplane pilots. Less appreciated are the risks of touching down in a tail-high attitude, which are particularly

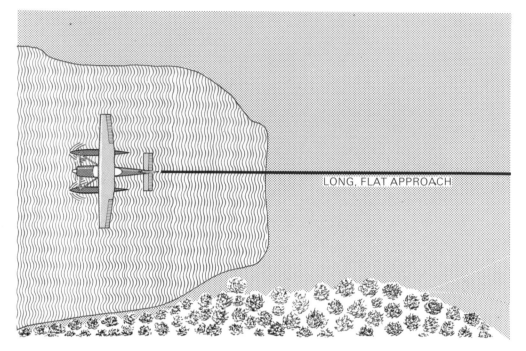

LONG, FLAT APPROACH

Fig. 68: Landing tail-high, following a flat approach. If the bows enter the water first there is a risk of one or both floats pulling into the water (see lower picture, Fig. 67).

applicable to float-plane operations. The sequence of events is as follows (Fig. 68):

1.   The aircraft is alighting under glassy water conditions, consequently a long, flat, powered approach has preceded the actual touchdown.

2.   At the point of contact the aircraft is flown on to the water in a tail-high, nose-down attitude, causing the front portions of the floats to enter the water first.

3.   Because the front under-surface of the floats is similar in shape to an inverted airfoil there is an immediate tendency for the floats to be pulled hard into the water (see Fig. 67 on page 207).

4.   By now the seaplane's centre of gravity is behind the point of water

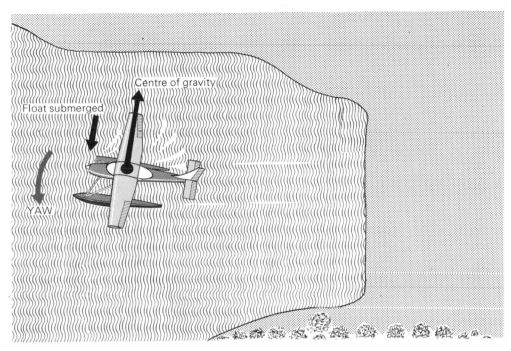

Fig. 69: The seaplane equivalent of wheelbarrowing. When one float tends to pull into the water (for reasons explained in Figs. 67 and 68) a combination of uneven drag and a tendency for the centre of gravity to take over can cause a violent swing. The wing will then go down, enter the water and create the risk of capsizing.

contact and the slightest yaw (caused by a crosswind, rudder movement or one float hitting a wave) will provoke a swing that is similar in nature to a wheelbarrowing landplane (Fig. 69).

If this situation is allowed to get out of hand the seaplane will very likely turn over. If you do inadvertently touch down on the bows of the floats get the power off, ease the stick or wheel gently back and settle the floats into the water. The fact that you have arrived high-tailed and bow-happy will almost certainly mean that the airspeed is rather higher than it should be for comfort. A bounce may result from your attempts at stopping the floatplane from becoming a submarine, but that is as naught compared with the implications of capsizing.

When the water is rough

All seaplanes have wave height limits and only experience will teach how to recognize these from the air while making the inspection run. The obvious precaution one should take is to aim for an arrival in the most sheltered area of water. Aim to touch down in a more nose-up attitude than usual and be prepared to use power in settling down after a possible bounce. If the seaplane starts porpoising, on no account hang around.to see if it will get better or worse. Go round again and have another try.

Engine failure over land

In the case of amphibians an engine failure over land should be dealt with as in any other landplane. Floatplanes do not always enjoy the luxury of a retractable landing gear but, given reasonably flat ground, they can be forced landed without too much damage.

Aim to touch down with the keels of the floats parallel to the ground. If the nose is held too high the heels will make contact first, cause the seaplane to pitch forward and perhaps dig in the bows. Immediately contact is made with the ground the stick/wheel must be brought fully back to discourage the 'plane from standing on its nose.

The real professional never stops learning about flying, and this is particularly true of seaplane operations. Apart from their generally poor handling qualities seaplanes are themselves very like landplanes, but understanding the ever-changing water is a skill that really sorts out the competent from the 'also rans'.

11. BE KIND TO YOUR ENGINE

The most expensive single item in a one-motor 'plane is the engine. And on it depends whether you stay up or have to come down. Yet this vital part of the aircraft is not always treated with sympathy and respect, partly because its particular weaknesses are sometimes not understood. Occasionally there are other reasons – like 'this club 'plane is costing me a fortune so why not hammer the engine and get there quickly'. But there are other ways of shortening the life of an engine, some of them far more damaging than the simple act of 'firewalling' the throttle in an effort to save a few minutes on the journey (or the cost of hiring). What these anti-social gentlemen fail to realize is that some poor soul has to fly the aircraft after they have finished wringing it out.

Most of the following hints for happy engines relate to the piston variety since they are more vulnerable to damage through mismanagement than are gas turbines. In any case, by the time a pilot has graduated to flying turboprops or jets one likes to think he has attained a degree of professionalism calculated to reject callous engine handling like the Bubonic Plague.

The larger, geared and turbocharged piston-engines have a life (TBO) of around 1400 hours. Life tends to become longer as engines become less complex and of lower power, 2000 hours being achieved by many of the particularly reliable units. Most airworthiness authorities are prepared to grant one, and perhaps two, 10 per cent extensions, particularly if relatively minor replacements (like new piston rings) have been made. So ideally our 2000-hour engine could, with careful use and good management, run for 2400 hours before it must be swapped for a reconditioned unit.

Not all engines get one, let alone two extensions. Indeed some fail to make their certified TBO. Why? There are a few cases of below standard engines but, in the main, life has been shortened by poor engine handling. Before describing some of these pilot-induced engine diseases a word about the anatomy of the piston-engine might be of value.

Nuts, bolts and engine anatomy

For all his engineering skill mankind has failed to invent a metal or alloy that will serve for all purposes. For example, good quality steel, ideal for highly stressed components like crankshafts, connecting rods and camshafts, is totally unsuitable for pistons. For one thing steel is too heavy; the vibration that would result from fitting steel pistons would be good for the liver but bad for everything else. Less obviously, a hard steel piston running up and down an equally hard steel or cast iron cylinder would soon cause excessive friction and probably seize. So a special aluminium alloy has been developed for pistons. It is light and hard-wearing as, strangely, it is the walls of the cylinder that alter their dimensions after a time, not the much softer aluminium pistons. But it does not end with aluminium and steel; there are special alloys for the bearings, some based on bronze (a mixture of copper and tin), and some made from varieties of steel, each of which has a particular talent.

We are, of course, lucky to have at our disposal all these wonderful metals but the problem is that they not only differ in properties but they also expand at different rates when heated, and this is one of the most important causes of premature wear.

Warming up and running down

If you do not believe me when I talk of expansion and contraction, stand

by the engine of your favourite 'plane after it has been shut down and listen
to the ticks and clicks as it cools. That hot, expanded metal is contracting,
not all of it at the same rate, and some pretty irresistible stresses occur as a
result.

To cater for expansion of the various parts engine designers allow
clearances between, for example, the valves and their guides, the pistons
and the cylinders and the gaps in the piston rings. These clearances are all
carefully calculated and the various parts are machined to fine limits of
accuracy. But these provisions for expansion will only protect the engine
so long as it is allowed to reach its working temperature gradually. So the
first lesson on the subject of being kind to your engine is this:

> Never attempt a run-up before the engine has had ample time to
> reach a working temperature.

How long is ample time? The aircraft manual should give guidance
here. Oil temperature is usually a non-starter because on most aircraft it
will refuse to enter the 'green sector' until after take-off. Cylinder head
temperature is probably a better guide but in the absence of specific
advice think in terms of a five-minute warm-up in moderate climates and
up to double that time when the temperature is below freezing. Naturally
much of this time can be spent taxiing to the holding point. There is no
need to sit there terrified to move off.

At the end of the trip it is equally important not to shut down a hot
engine immediately, particularly when the ambient temperature is near
or below freezing. Allow the engine to idle at around 1000 RPM (a good
opportunity to test that both mags are still working) and after about five
minutes, when the engine has come down to an even temperature, it
should then be safe to pull the ICO and shut down. Here again, much if
not all of the five minutes may be devoted to taxiing in at the end of the
trip. But the damage is done when pilots land, park within a minute or so
and then switch off a hot engine on a cold day. That is how cylinder heads
are cracked.

These two simple elements of engine handling can, on their own, add
many hours to its life.

The function of oil

Ask the average person the purpose of pouring oil into engines and he will probably tell you it is there to lubricate. That, of course, is perfectly true. For without a film of oil to separate fast moving parts they would soon generate so much friction that bits of the engine would weld themselves together. When this happens, usually through loss of oil pressure or because there is no oil, we say the engine has 'seized'. However, important as it is, the lubricating function of oil is only part of the deal. In addition the engine oil does the following:

1. It assists the piston rings in forming a gas tight seal within the cylinder walls.

2. It dissipates heat generated by moving parts that, unlike the cylinder, have no direct access to air cooling.

3. It acts as a detergent and removes carbon, acid and minute metal deposits from where they might cause damage. Much of this rubbish is a bi-product of combustion but some of it is powdered engine wear. The worst of it is deposited in the oil filter but to convince yourself that the oil does a good job at keeping the works bright and shiny compare its colour when you pour it in with what comes out when the time arrives to drain the sump.

It will be clear from all this that modern engine oils are something of a technological achievement. Various additives are introduced to prevent ash forming in the high working temperatures of engines and so forth. In fact special oils have been developed for all manner of piston, diesel and turbine engines. The message therefore is that you must ensure that the correct grade of oil is used in your engine. And that includes using the right oil for summer or winter operation. Because if you get careless about it the wrong oil could land you with the cost of a new engine – or worse if there is a spectacular power failure at an inconvenient moment.

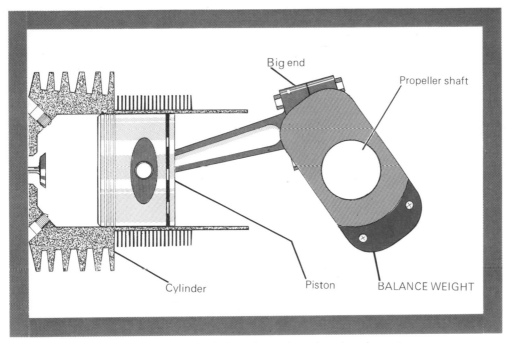

Fig. 70: Crankshaft balance weights. Imagine the damage these can cause within the engine when they break loose following prolonged misuse of the engine controls.

Piston-engine handling

Here are some of the more common examples of bad engine handling that one sees in the course of testing pilots. Individually they probably do little damage, particularly when perpetrated for short periods. Collectively they can materially shorten the life of an engine.

Harsh use of throttle

As the pistons run back and forth in their cylinders and pedal around the crankshaft a fair amount of metal is moving at high speed, coming to an immediate halt and then doing an about turn. To dampen the vibration that would otherwise result from all this mechanical violence balance weights are fitted to the crankshaft (Fig. 70) and judging from the relative smoothness of modern engines they seem to do a pretty good job.

Flying around as they do these balance weights give their retaining bolts something of a beating. Not only do they try to fly off as the crank rotates at 2500–3600 RPM (according to engine type) but they are also subjected to acceleration and deceleration forces when the pilot opens and closes the throttle. Harsh movement of the throttle will provoke the engine into changing speed in a like manner and repeated treatment of this kind has been known to make the balance weights depart. When they do leave the crankshaft all manner of expensive mischief is caused as lumps of solid metal graunch around inside the engine.

So when you simulate an engine failure during training, refrain from snapping shut the throttle because back pressure will cause rapid deceleration of hard-working parts and you will be at risk of flinging balance weights from where they belong. Likewise when overshoot action is required, *ease* the throttle gently open while adding power.

Smooth operation of the throttle is particularly important when flying aerobatics. Because then, in addition to all the other strains, your tortured engine must suffer complex gyroscopic precession forces as the aircraft goes through the unnatural, nose falling sideways, engine following a corkscrew path or describing a vertical loop in the air.

Incorrect use of the mixture control

The ideal fuel/air mixture in a ratio of approximately one to fifteen (by weight) progressively changes as the aircraft climbs and air density decreases. So the mixture control is used to lean the brew, prevent a sooty engine and ensure economic operation. We talk about leaning the mixture but in fact all we are doing is maintaining the ideal fuel/air ratio which has been carefully set by the manufacturers for sea level conditions.

Correct use of the mixture control can make a very considerable difference to fuel consumption. However, it should be remembered that in principle a rich mixture causes the engine to run cool while a lean fuel/air mix raises the temperature. If one over-leans the mixture the engine temperature can easily rise to the point of danger. In an effort to economize on fuel costs some pilots misguidedly go heavy on the mixture control and end up spending several times what they have saved in fuel on engine repairs.

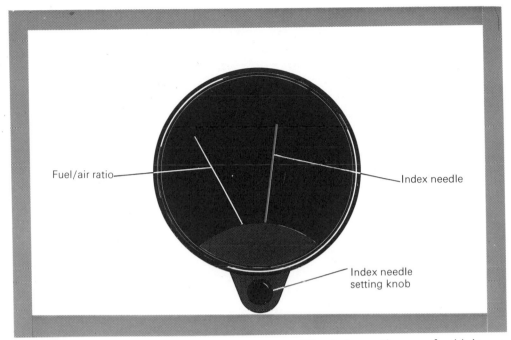

Fig. 71: The engine gas temperature gauge. The information on fuel/air ratio provided by these instruments is invaluable for fine setting of the mixture. The index finger and its setting knob are used to provide a datum for the EGT needle. No scale is provided because optimum readings vary according to cruising level, ambient temperature etc.

Operation of the mixture control is simple enough. You set up the engine then lean the mixture until slight rough running accompanied by a modest drop in RPM announces that you have overdone it. At this point you carefully move the mixture control back towards RICH until rough running ceases and the original RPM are restored. The engine should now be properly adjusted for optimum fuel economy, but as an added safeguard it is good practice to monitor the cylinder head temperature at regular intervals. If it shows signs of approaching the red line on no account wait for things to start cooking; adjust the mixture towards rich and bring down the temperature.

Additional facilities may be provided in the aircraft to assist in fuel management:

a) Fuel/air ratio meter: This gauge, which functions by measuring the exhaust gas temperature, has an index pointer which can be moved with a little knob (Fig. 71). The mixture should be leaned until the ratio needle is at its peak. (The index needle is moved to follow the ratio indicator and so provide a datum.) At the peak setting the mixture should then be enriched slightly by adjusting the mixture control until the ratio needle has backed a fraction from the index needle. Unfortunately the index cannot be left in that position for future use because its position changes according to altitude and other considerations such as air temperature, which are outside the control of the pilot. So remember, if you climb, descend or increase the power setting the mixture control will require your most careful attention.

b) Fuel flow meter: When your 'plane is powered by a fuel-injected engine the manifold pressure gauge will incorporate fuel flow readings in gallons (or litres) per hour. The aircraft manual will give RPM/manifold pressure settings for various power outputs (i.e. percentage maximum power), at different altitudes. Some thoughtful manufacturers even display a table of these figures in the aircraft. Armed with these figures, which also quote gallons per hour against each power setting, it is a simple matter to adjust the mixture control until the correct reading appears on the fuel flow meter.

Since it samples the exhaust gases, and is therefore in a position to gauge with accuracy the state of the mixture being burned in the engine, the fuel/air ratio meter is often fitted to aircraft even when they sport a fuel flow indicator. So when you have the two instruments at your disposal fine adjustment of the mixture can be made with the aid of the fuel/air ratio meter. A little extra care in setting up the mixture can over a period save a great deal of fuel and help maintain your engine in good health.

Incorrect use of throttle and propeller controls

Astonishing as it may seem, although the constant speed propeller has been with us since 1938 or even earlier some modern pilots have never learned to operate it properly. In many respects the variable pitch element of a modern propeller is very similar in purpose to a car gearbox. Force a low power vehicle up a hill in top and the engine will labour. Keep up the ill treatment and very likely it will overheat and start knocking.

By applying too high a throttle setting when coarse pitch (i.e. low RPM) has been selected an aero-engine can be made to labour in exactly the same way. There are times, particularly while training, when full throttle may have to be applied – stall recovery and missed approach procedures being two examples. Before such exercises it is vitally important to ensure that firewalling the throttle will not make the engine come up against a wrongly set propeller, as this is equivalent to flogging a little-engined car up a steep hill in top gear. The aircraft manual should quote the minimum propeller setting for full throttle. Usually it is 2400 RPM.

With engines of low power the risk of fully opening the throttle into a propeller set at too coarse a pitch is slight. But pilots of little aircraft often graduate to bigger and more complex hardware, some of it with turbo-charged engines, that will certainly suffer a lot of harm if abused. On the basis that good habits formed today will look after us tomorrow pilots of even the lowest-powered light 'planes fitted with constant speed propellers should form the habit of changing power in this way:

a) Increasing power: Increase propeller RPM first, then open the throttle but not beyond maximum manifold pressure allowed for that engine speed.

b) Decreasing power: Decrease throttle setting to the required manifold pressure first then reduce propeller RPM to the appropriate speed but not below the minimum allowed for that manifold pressure.

This procedure may easily be remembered by the little saying:

'Rev up and throttle back.'

Naturally the mixture will need adjusting and when it has been leaned at cruising level it is essential to select RICH before applying climbing power.

The pilot who enjoys the fruits of careful engine management is the one who checks all temperatures and pressures, RPM, fuel flow and everything else at regular intervals. Because some readings affect others (for example a change in RPM will alter the manifold pressure) fine adjustment of throttle, propeller and mixture controls may be needed throughout the flight.

Turbocharger techniques

The common or garden piston-engine is a dishonest beast. You pump in expensive fuel expecting a fair return in horsepower, only to find that most of it has been completely wasted. Engine efficiency may be regarded under three headings: thermal, mechanical and volumetric. These words are not as forbidding as they may sound. In essence thermal efficiency means this. One can calculate the amount of heat energy in a given quantity of fuel (expressed in BTUs) and through simple arithmetic convert that into power. Astonishing as it may seem the average, normally aspirated piston-engine uses only 25–30 per cent of the available heat energy for conversion into power. The remaining 70–75 per cent is wasted. In terms of mechanical efficiency at least 10 per cent and perhaps as much as 15 per cent of the miserable amount of power we get from our energetic fuel goes in driving the oil, hydraulic and vacuum pumps along with the generator. Internal friction within the engine also contributes to this loss. The piston-engine is not all that marvellous at breathing and is in fact only capable of filling its cylinders by 75–85 per cent.

All this is bad enough when the engine is confined to the ground. But give it wings and its borderline volumetric efficiency is further eroded by the decrease in air density that occurs with altitude. Some of these deficiencies can be balanced by forcing mixture under pressure into the cylinders, a process long known as supercharging. It is done for two reasons:

a) To increase power above that possible when the engine is normally aspirated.

b) To compensate for the decrease in air density with height and so enable the engine to maintain its rated power while flying at high altitudes.

The practice is often called 'boosting' and it may be accomplished by fitting a geared supercharger which is driven by the engine crankshaft, or it can take the form of a blower driven by a small turbine which obtains its power from the exhaust gases. The geared supercharger is heavy, less accomplished at maintaining engine power over a wide range of altitudes and expensive. Although it provides more immediate power changes with throttle movement than the turbine type (widely known as a turbocharger) the disadvantages outweigh their advantages and geared superchargers are now confined to engines of earlier design.

It is sometimes thought that the turbocharger gives us something for nothing in so far as it reclaims exhaust energy and turns it into power, but this is not the case. By introducing a turbine in the exhaust system, back pressure is generated and the engine is actually robbed of a little power. Fortunately this is more than balanced by the effects of forcing mixture under pressure into cylinders that would otherwise never be more than 75–85 per cent full.

To illustrate the advantages of turbocharging as a means of maintaining power at altitude take a look at these figures. They relate to a pair of engines in the 200hp bracket, one normally aspirated, the other turbocharged:

Altitude feet	Maximum horsepower	
	normally aspirated	turbocharged
20,000	99	150
15,000	122	187
10,000	148	215
5,000	177	210
Sea Level	210	200

Of course there is a lot more to turbochargers than a simple turbine driving a blower. To discourage the system from over-boosting its engine at low cruising levels a quite complex arrangement of waste gates and valves is provided to control blower output. The degree of automation varies from one system to the next and I shall therefore only describe their management in general terms.

Handling turbochargers

The simplest turbochargers have no automatic manifold pressure control and are capable of over-boosting the engine at low levels. Particularly during take-off care must be exercised not to exceed the maximum permitted manifold pressure. This is usually 'red lined' on the gauge but in addition it is the practice to fit over-boost warning lights which come on when over-enthusiastic use of the throttle(s) is about to blow up the engine(s). Serious damage can be caused by prolonged over-boosting and, although one has better things to watch during take-off, the manifold pressure gauges must on no account be ignored. Many pilots like to open up to take-off power on the brakes, then release the anchor and concentrate on keeping straight. Whatever your feelings on the matter, and in my view it is possible if inconvenient to open the throttles to the correct setting while moving, the red line must not be violated.

Turbochargers of this kind do not always provide automatic control during the climb so as altitude is gained manifold pressure will have to be maintained by advancing the throttle in the usual, normally aspirated way. Obviously fully automatic systems have over-boost protection and the manifold pressure remains constant until the aircraft climbs to an altitude beyond the capabilities of the blower.

Throttle response

The turbine/compressor assembly rotates at tens of thousands of RPM and it therefore takes time to change speed by, say, 5000 RPM or more. There is therefore an appreciable time lag between moving the throttle and obtaining a settled reading on the manifold pressure gauge (although modern turbochargers have improved on earlier designs in this respect). So to obtain the best from turbocharged engines and to avoid chasing the manifold pressure needle up and down its scale, all throttle movements must be slow and gradual.

Much damage can result from prolonged descents at very low power settings. The engine is allowed to cool, then at the new cruising level, when the metalwork is almost stone cold, the tap is opened and power demanded at a time when the working clearances are all wrong. It is important not to treat any engine in this manner, but such abuse is particularly damaging to turbocharged engines. Prolonged descents must be made 'power on' to ensure maintenance of a reasonable working temperature.

Shutting down turbocharged engines

At the end of the trip when you have taxied in the turbocharger will continue rotating at its countless thousands of revs. It is not generally realized that when the engine is shut down the supply of oil to this fast-spinning gadget ceases. So to avoid expensive replacements spare a moment or two at the parking lot while the works wind down. A good pilot does that in kindness to any engine, but when the aircraft is turbocharged add a few more moments of idling time while the turbine calms down.

Turboprops

By the time they are prepared to let you loose on turboprop aircraft you have probably already absorbed the recurring plea of this book for more professionalism, since turboprop and jet pilots must, of necessity, attain high standards of knowledge, skill and airmanship. In addition, turboprop (and jet) engines have become so reliable and simple to operate that there is little to tell, so to some extent this section can do no more than satisfy the curiosity of strictly piston-engine pilots by highlighting a few problem areas (there are not many) related to turboprop engine operation.

Types of turboprop engines

The two main classes of turboprop engines are the fixed-shaft (e.g. Garrett AiResearch) which has one compressor/turbine assembly rotating on a common assembly, and free turbine units of which the PT6 is an example. These have a compressor/turbine assembly, known as a gas generator, which does not have any direct connection to the propeller. A separate power turbine, supplied with pressure flow by the gas generator, is connected to the propeller. In both engine types a reduction gear is necessary to convert what may be approaching 50,000 (yes, fifty thousand) turbine

RPM to less than 3000 propeller RPM. In simplified form the two engine types are illustrated in Figs 72 and 73.

Because the free turbine engine has two independent shafts, two RPM indicators are provided for the pilot and while terminology has yet to be standardized the turbine driving the propeller is often known as N_1 while that forming part of the gas generator is called N_2. It is the practice to start and shut down free turbine engines with their propellers feathered.

Among the engine instruments provided for turboprops are the RPM indicator(s) already mentioned (calibrated in percentage of maximum), torque meter (which sometimes has an additional scale indicating horse-power being delivered to the propeller), interstage turbine temperature (known in the trade as ITT), fuel flow in pounds or kilogrammes per hour, oil pressure and oil temperature.

Starting

Some engines require the high pressure cock (usually incorporated with the fuel condition lever) to be opened after the starter has spun up the engine to 10–12 per cent RPM. Advancing the condition lever to the GROUND position allows fuel to enter the spray nozzles and ignition should occur almost instantly. This will be confirmed by a rise in temperature on the ITT which should carefully be watched for signs of a hot start. If the needle threatens to exceed the red line, shut down immediately or you may cook the engine. Hot starts are rare these days. But they can be expensive. After the engine has settled into ground idle the starter is switched to the generator position. Before attempting to light up the other engine it is important to check the battery state for recovery (voltmeter) and, in the case of ni-cad units, their temperature. These otherwise excellent batteries have been known to over-heat and blow a hole in the side of the fuselage.

Some aircraft have fully automatic starting whereby all that is required of the pilot is to energize the starters and watch the dials.

Whether or not one should start both engines prior to taxiing depends on the type of aircraft. The Embraer Xingu, for example, is cleared for taxiing on one engine. All turboprops taxi as though there is a bomb behind them unless full use is made of the 'Beta' range (i.e. propeller manually controlled to provide near zero thrust). This can be noisy for the passengers

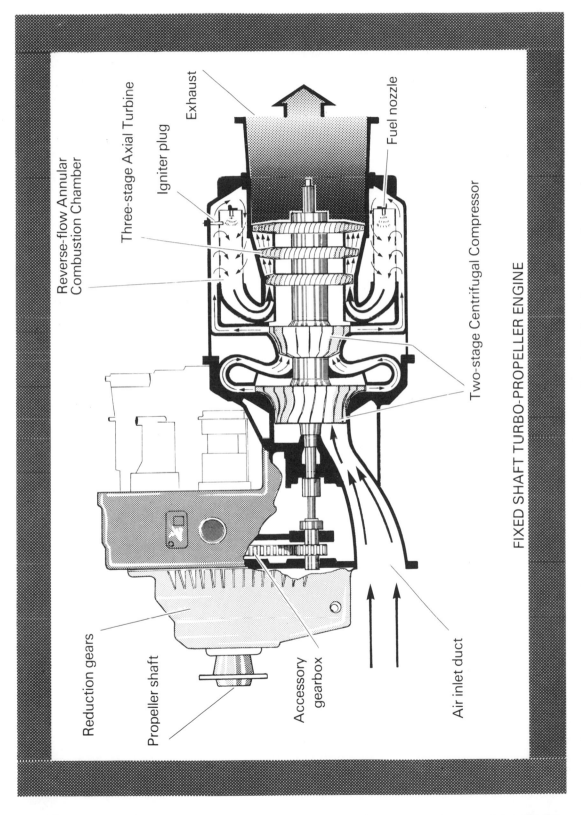

Reduction gears

Reverse-flow Annular Combustion Chamber

Three-stage Axial Turbine

Igniter plug

Exhaust

Fuel nozzle

Two-stage Centrifugal Compressor

Propeller shaft

Accessory gearbox

Air inlet duct

FIXED SHAFT TURBO-PROPELLER ENGINE

Fig. 72: Simplified illustration of a typical Garrett AiResearch fixed shaft turbo-propeller engine. Fixed guide vanes have been omitted for clarity.

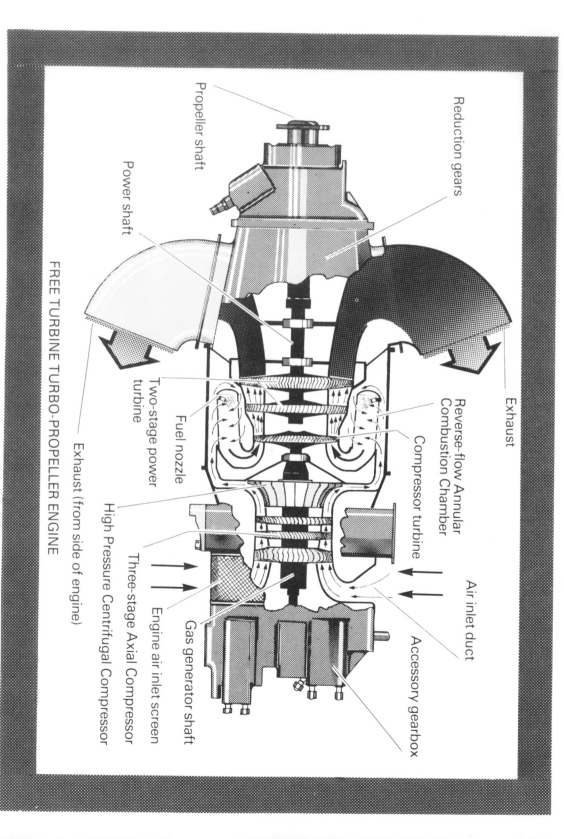

Fig. 73: Simplified illustration of a typical Pratt and Whitney two shaft, free turbine turbo-propeller engine. Fixed guide vanes have been omitted for clarity.

FREE TURBINE TURBO-PROPELLER ENGINE

Reduction gears

Propeller shaft

Power shaft

Exhaust

Two-stage power turbine

Fuel nozzle

Reverse-flow Annular Combustion Chamber

Compressor turbine

Exhaust (from side of engine)

High Pressure Centrifugal Compressor

Three-stage Axial Compressor

Engine air inlet screen

Gas generator shaft

Air inlet duct

Accessory gearbox

and on level ground aircraft with free turbine engines can comfortably be taxied on the exhaust alone with the propellers feathered.

Take-off
Some of the Garrett AiResearch engines are fitted with torque limiters which prevent risk of propeller transmission damage through using excessive power at low levels. Since not all engines enjoy this facility care must be exercised at low levels, particularly during take-off, to ensure that torque limits are not exceeded. These are marked as a red line on the torque meters.

In the cruise
At high altitudes it is possible, through adopting too great a power setting, to over-heat turboprop engines and while some of the Garrett AiResearch units have temperature limiters most power units do not. The ITT gauge is provided to help avoid over-cooking your engine and to assist in accurate power setting. Make full use of it.

Reverse thrust
Reverse thrust is a valuable aid to shortening the post-landing run. However, it must be used with discretion.

1.　Never apply reverse thrust until the nosewheel is on the ground.

2.　Take care not to overheat the engine by excessive use. A glance at the ITT while reverse thrust is in operation will on some aircraft reveal how quickly the temperature can rise when this is selected.

Taxiing backwards
One of the party pieces of turboprop aircraft is their ability to taxi backwards. There may be exceptional circumstances when this rather lunatic talent can be put to good effect but in the main it is best regarded as an act reserved for air displays.

If, for special reasons, it is important for you to 'go astern' here are two little hints that could save you a little embarrassment and a lot of cash:

1. Since it is almost impossible to see behind the aircraft, have someone on the ground to marshal you.

2. Application of brake while in reverse can very easily sit the bird on its tail. So there are two things to remember –
    a) Taxi backwards very slowly.
    b) Apply the brakes very gently.

The fruits of engine kindness

A very old airline captain, long since retired, was interviewed on television; it was his ninetieth birthday. 'Looking back,' the interviewer started, 'do you have any regrets about your life?' The old four-ringer thought a little and replied, 'Well, if I had known how long I was going to live, I'd have looked after myself better.'

Most of us cannot guess how long we shall live, except on the rough basis of life expectancy statistics. The figure very much depends on our living conditions, style of life and the avoidance of self-inflicted damage. Engines are not unlike humans in these respects. Experience tells us what average life to expect and we know that this can be achieved or even exceeded by the avoidance of pilot-inflicted damage. Engine life can be influenced by the type of operation (sand plays havoc with all engines) but, except when there is a case of faulty manufacture, the service given by piston, turboprop or jet engines is largely determined by the pilots and engineers who manage them.

12. IN CONCLUSION

On reading this book, newly qualified or relatively inexperienced pilots may form the view that flying is too complex by half, too exacting a discipline and best left to the professionals. While I would be the first to agree that there is much to learn I certainly do not want to create the impression that pilots must be supermen. It is not in any way the purpose of this book to discourage, but rather the opposite.

The 'know it all' pilots will no doubt accuse me of being alarmist and of seeing dangers that do not exist, but the accident statistics and the details that go with them prove my case. Most skilful, well-balanced pilots will agree that the average level of flying skill and airmanship could be a lot better in both the light and general aviation sectors, and will recognize that the danger areas mentioned in this book are real enough.

It is a well known aviation fact that if you get six pilots (particularly instructors) to discuss a problem they will come up with seven answers. And in the eyes of most aviators the 'standard' way of doing things is the method used by them. While one should not be too ready to insist on absolute conformity in every detail the merits of standardization are acknowledged by most responsible flying training authorities. The various procedures described in this book are, with few exceptions, not flying training exercises, i.e. such basic subjects as taking off, stalling, and the effects of controls. Their aim is rather to highlight common weaknesses among pilots and give advice on how to do better, in the hope of improving skill and reducing the accident rate.

Few of us see ourselves as do others, and very few pilots see their flying through the eyes of their passengers. I have often made a point of inviting rough pilots to sit quietly and watch while I reproduce some of their particular brand of poor handling. 'Do I really fly like that?' they ask in utter disbelief as though hearing their own voice on a tape recorder for the first time. I once tried this technique with a pilot who flew some of the worst aerobatics in my experience (how do you induce negative 'g' all the way round a barrel roll?). When I copied what he had just done he was promptly sick.

Not seeing ourselves as do others may, in everyday life, cause us disappointment (because we rate our own abilities too highly) or provoke clashes of personality. But this same human frailty in a pilot can lose him more than popularity. If he is ham-fisted on the controls his reputation will deter others from flying with him. If excessive self-esteem is allowed to take charge, bad habits easily grow into dangerous ones and then there is no end of trouble in store for the pilot himself, his unfortunate passengers and perhaps innocents on the ground.

With these and other thoughts in mind the aviation authorities of the world require their professional pilots to undergo regular checks. In South Africa, for example, you are re-tested for your instrument rating every six months. The British test their instructors at two-yearly intervals while airline flight deck crews have route checks, base checks and many others. Air forces are particularly strict about checking their pilots. Military they may be; professional they most certainly are. In view of all this it is strange that only amateur pilots expect to go about their flying without question, free from the critical eye of an experienced examiner who after a relatively short check ride could probably stop future problems before it is too late. The professional sitting on the flight deck of a transport 'plane has enjoyed very much higher standards of training than the private pilot (or even the majority of those in general aviation), he may have 15,000–20,000 or more hours yet this pundit at the top of his profession goes for his regular checks in the right spirit. He is not too proud to place himself on the line. In contrast, many amateurs are affronted when it is suggested that a check ride might be to their advantage.

In the USA the authorities have in fact introduced two-yearly checks for private pilots and while they have proved only partially successful (possibly because the form of the test has not been closely enough specified) it is nevertheless a step in the right direction.

Having outlined the evils of self congratulation and over confidence it must now be said that man has another, paradoxical side to his character which is his tendency to underestimate what he can achieve through good training and diligent practice. The ability to gain skills of all kinds is, to a considerable extent, dependent upon your attitude to difficulties and imagined difficulties. Technical subjects are not black magic. They are, in most cases, simple common sense principles applied in the right direction. Difficult procedures, where a number of separate actions have to be made simultaneously, should be regarded as a challenge that can be conquered under the two-prong attack of good instruction and intelligent practice. Complex drills which require a number of control actions in preparation for the next phase of flight should not be dismissed as 'for the professionals'. They should be learned as a mnemonic or carefully executed with the aid of a checklist.

When correct attitudes are allied to regular checks with a competent pilot the way is clear for you to be a better pilot. And when everyone is of a like mind the reduction in the accident rate will be dramatic indeed.

INDEX